Praise for the first edition of *Effective Business Writing*:

"The uniqueness of *Effective Business Writing* is the clarity of its form, style, and substance."

—McAdory Lipscomb, Executive Vice President, Showtime Networks

"Throughout the book the author practices what she preaches; she writes simply and clearly and breaks up the text so it's easy to find the major points."

—*Writing Concepts*

"This book is a 'must have' for anyone who writes in business. It covers a wide range of topics in a clear, readable style, and it provides excellent examples of well-written letters and memos."

—Stever Robbins, Research Associate, Harvard Business School

"Reading the chapter on process was a breakthrough for me. Now I draft quickly and come back later to revise."

—William Neacy, Senior Market Research Analyst, DuPont Merck Pharmaceutical Company

"Excellent helpful hints for getting over writer's block."

—Randi Lattman, Training Director, Viacom Inc.

Effective Business Writing

Effective Business Writing

A GUIDE FOR THOSE WHO
WRITE ON THE JOB

Second Edition, Revised and Updated

MARYANN V. PIOTROWSKI

HarperPerennial

A Division of HarperCollinsPublishers

HarperCollins books may be purchased for educational, business, or sales promotional use. For information, please write: Special Markets Department, HarperCollins Publishers, Inc., 10 East 53rd Street, New York, NY 10022.

FIRST EDITION

Designed by Irving Perkins Associates, Inc.

Library of Congress Cataloging-in-Publication Data

Piotrowski, Maryann V.
  [Re: Writing]
  Effective business writing: a guide for those who write on the job / Maryann V. Piotrowski.—2nd ed., rev. and updated.
    p. cm.
  Includes index.
  ISBN 0-06-273381-8
  1. Business writing. I. Title.
HF5718.3.P56   1996
808'.066651—dc20   95-46256

96 97 98 99 00 ❖/HC 10 9 8 7 6 5 4

For my mother, a word person

Contents

Acknowledgments

My friends and business colleagues deserve credit and thanks for helping me craft this edition of the book. Writing is a lonely activity, but I broke the tedium by calling upon them. Some of them provided feedback on chapters I had just written; some provided letters or memos for my book; some provided encouragement. All of them were generous with their time and ideas.

Thanks to you all: Susan Broadribb, Benjamin Hayes, Paul Heinerscheid, Alexander Hood, Joan Kertis, Steve Kinnal, Patricia Lambe, Cynthia Livingston, Eleanor Livingston, Jennifer Mapes, Christopher Montpetit, Philip McCarron, Janet McDougall, Nan McNamara, Kurt Rao, Roger Richards, Stever Robbins, Phyllis Strimling, Dolores Sullivan, Barbara Swartz.

I also wish to thank those organizations that allowed me to use their letters or memos in my book: New York University School of Law, Radcliffe College, Satellite Network Systems, Showtime Networks, Times Publishing Company, United Way of Pelham, Washington Metropolitan Area Transit Authority.

Finally, thanks to Buz Wyeth, executive editor at HarperCollins, for his suggestions, support, and good humor.

Preface to the Second Edition

If you were asked what job-related tasks you most dislike, would writing be on your list? If so, you are not unusual. Many others in industry, the public sector, and the professions dislike writing. They find that they spend too much time writing, and, when they finally send out a document, neither they, their bosses, nor their readers find it effective.

Yet the ability to write well is an important skill—and one that brings you great visibility. Just as you judge others by their writing, so too others judge you by your writing. The memos, letters, and reports you write provide powerful evidence of your overall competence and of your management style.

This book will help you improve your writing. You can read it from cover to cover, or you can use it as a reference book.

It represents a distillation of what I've learned about business writing from several different perspectives: as an executive in banking and finance; as a writing instructor at the Harvard Business School and at the John F. Kennedy School of Government, Massachusetts Institute of Technology's Sloan School of Management, Boston College, and Boston University; and as a communications consultant to such clients as Time Warner Inc., Viacom Inc., Showtime Networks Inc., DuPont Merck Pharmaceutical Company, *St. Petersburg Times, Congressional Quarterly,* General Cinema, Condé Nast Publications Inc., Discovery Communications, Inc., and the U.S. Civil Service Commission.

My aim in this second edition is identical to my aim in the first: to provide readers with an up-to-date, clear, and concise guide to writing in today's business world. I have added some new chapters on goodwill letters, letters of request, sales letters, and international correspondence, and I have provided updated sample letters for many of the other chapters. I have also dropped a couple of chapters and have revised portions of most of the remaining chapters.

My hope is that those of you who know the first edition will find this edition faithful to the first, but newer and better. For those of you who are first-time readers, I hope this edition will help you become more competent—and more confident—writers.

Maryann V. Piotrowski
Cambridge, Massachusetts
December, 1995

Effective Business Writing

Bad Writing Is Bad for Business

Efficiently run businesses cannot tolerate unclear memos, letters, and reports. Business stops, or is slowed, as a result of poor communication. Orders don't get delivered, or they don't get delivered on time; tasks don't get done, or they don't get done correctly. Productivity decreases, while labor and supervisory costs increase. The morale of employees suffers, as does the image of the firm.

William J. Gallagher, who was for many years Manager of Communication Services at Arthur D. Little, Inc., a major consulting company, has estimated that up to 30 percent of letters and memos in industry and government do nothing more than seek clarification of earlier correspondence or respond to that request for clarification. That estimate does not include the thousands of letters and memos that are not acted upon because they are unclear. Bad writing is bad for business.

Most people in business—employers and employees alike—agree that writing skills are weak. Some poor writing stems from a lack of instruction, or poor instruction, in our schools. But much poor writing comes about not because of a lack of schooling, but rather from attitudes held by the writers themselves or from limitations prevalent in the workplace.

SOME CAUSES OF POOR WRITING

One or more of the following causes may contribute to poor writing:

Ignoring the reader. Readers today want as much information as possible in as little time as possible. They want to know instantly what a piece of writing is about, and they want to understand it after one careful, but quick, reading. Writers who ignore their readers, sometimes quite unconsciously, do so by giving too much, too little, or the wrong kinds of information. They use specialized vocabulary that is unfamiliar to their readers; they bury their message in a style that is dense or bureaucratic, or both. They write without considering their readers' needs, interests, or opinions.

A *lack of professional pride*. Some people who write on the job do not consider writing to be part of their professional duties; therefore, they are unwilling to give it the time and discipline it requires. They are bankers, chemists, accountants, or marketing managers—not writers. Writing is a nuisance to them.

A *lack of confidence*. Writers who lack confidence rely on the file cabinet or computer disk to do much of their writing. They recycle old letters by borrowing paragraphs, moving around sentences, and changing a few words. They put together a "new" letter, but one that is, nonetheless, ineffective.

Inexperience. Since much business is conducted over the phone, at meetings, and in casual conversations, some employees lack writing experience. Even though they have learned basic writing skills in school, they have not had sufficient exposure to, or practice in, writing for business. The style of academic writing is different from that of business writing.

Writing for the wrong reasons. Some writers write to impress others rather than to express themselves clearly. They fear that they will not appear educated or knowledgeable unless they dip every word in gold, unless they embroider every sentence. Some of these writers are simply insecure. They camouflage their ideas lest they be questioned or attacked. Others are unseasoned. They do not yet realize that top executives do not need to adopt airs.

Strict requirements. Some writers do not write well because their bosses set strict requirements. One boss may demand what he or she is used to: "That's the way we've done it for years." Another may set limits: "I won't read anything over a page long." Yet another may impose his or her style on the writer: "'Commence' is a better word than 'begin.'"

IMPROVING WRITING SKILLS

Identifying the causes of poor writing is the first step toward eliminating it. Several practical solutions can help overcome the causes mentioned above:

- Considering one's reader.
- Accepting writing as part of one's professional responsibility.
- Obtaining instruction and gaining practice in writing.
- Adopting a simple, straightforward approach.
- Questioning unreasonable corporate norms.

These pragmatic solutions may be obvious, but what is not so obvious is the importance of corporate and individual commitment.

Corporate commitment. Companies that value good writing should communicate that value to their employees. Some companies do this by praising good writing and by circulating good examples within the company. Some companies review employees' writing as part of performance reviews, and some supervisors review correspondence before it is sent. They also encourage peer review and peer editing. Many companies offer writing courses within the firm or reimburse tuition for courses taken outside the company. If managers endorse good writing—and serve as good role models—most employees will make an effort to improve their own writing.

Individual commitment. People starting out in business are quick to identify the skills that will help them get ahead. In most sectors, the job market is highly competitive. Even veteran employees try to improve their skills and add new skills to their repertoire. They sign up for computer courses and they attend seminars on technical subjects. Many, too, see the value in improving their writing ability. Unless an individual makes this commitment, there is little hope of true improvement.

WRITING IS AN ESSENTIAL SKILL

With so many new skills to learn, is it really so important to master such a basic skill as writing? Yes, it is. The ability to write well is—and will continue to be—an essential business skill, especially in this "age of information."

In 1994, the National Center on the Educational Quality of the Workforce, in conjunction with the Bureau of the Census, conducted various surveys among U.S. employers. In one survey, 3,000 employers were asked to rate on a scale of 1 to 5 (5 being the highest) the factors they considered important when hiring non-supervisory or production workers. Of 11 factors, "communication skills" was rated second highest, with a 4.2 rating; "attitude" was rated highest at 4.6. Communication skills are important at every job level. In most organizations, their importance mounts as job responsibilities mount. At the managerial level, they become the paramount skill.

Writing is an important skill on the job and in life. As William Zinsser, writer, editor, and teacher, points out in his book *Writing to Learn*, "Far too many Americans are prevented from doing useful work because they have never learned to express themselves. Contrary to general belief, writing is not something only 'writers' do; writing is a basic skill for getting through life."

The workplace is very much a part of life, and writing is very much a part of the workplace. The ability to write well—clearly and concisely—is not an ancillary skill; it is an essential skill.

Good writing is good for business.

2

Getting Started

Gaining Control

When a writing deadline approaches, or when a client or superior says, "Get that letter to me by tomorrow," you simply must get started. First you have to gain control of yourself. Then you have to gain control of your topic.

Gaining control of yourself requires that you put your mind and energy to the task. You may have to subdue the panic that the time pressure and the difficulty of the task impose, or you may have to circumvent your own clever procrastination rituals.

Getting started might mean that you need to think more, or it might mean that you need only close the door, have your calls answered, and begin writing. Whatever it takes to discipline yourself, do it.

You'll also have to gain control of your ego. You may come to a subject with knowledge and opinions that differ from those of your reader, yet egocentrism may keep you from seriously considering the other person's point of view. Being aware of your reader's perspective will help you avoid false starts.

Gaining control of your topic means nothing more than defining the task. Until you know what you have to do, you cannot begin doing it. The following methodical approach might help you overcome inertia and focus on the task. Ask yourself these questions:

PURPOSE: Am I writing to inquire, inform, persuade, motivate, or do I have more than one purpose?
                Besides writing to convey my thoughts, do I have some personal or political agenda? To go on record? To protect myself? To gain visibility?

SCOPE: Given my needs and my readers' needs, how much information should I include?

CONTENTS: What kinds of information will help me achieve my purpose?
                Do I have all the information I need?
                How, or where, can I get additional information?

CONSTRAINTS: What can work against me, or make my task more difficult? Time or cost constraints? My reader's attitudes? My own lack of credibility?

By answering questions like these, your task will become less amorphous, more concrete. As you gain control and get involved in the task, your lethargy will fade and your energy will build.

Seeing the Message Through Your Reader's Eyes

Put yourself in your reader's place and look at the world, and your message, through that person's eyes. This simple technique can help you get started on a project and, ultimately, write a document that is effective.

If your boss's desk is piled high with paper because it's a busy time of year, you may want to think twice about sending a long memo that may not get read, however important the matter is to you. Instead, consider sending a short one that gives the essentials—no more. If a customer points out that she is having trouble comparing and deciding upon one of several service contracts your company offers, write a simple follow-up letter comparing the contracts.

If you do not give your readers the right amount of information, if you do not write at their level of understanding, if you do not respond to their mood, your message may be ignored—or you may have to write yet another memo or letter on the same topic.

Before you write, ask yourself these questions about your reader:

How interested in the subject is the reader?
How knowledgeable is he or she about the subject?
What is my reader's purpose for reading? To make a decision? To be
    better informed?
Does my reader have special concerns or strong views about the subject?
    What are they?
How does my reader regard me personally and professionally?
What is my reader's style of doing business?
Will my reader pass this document on to others? Should I also consider
    their needs?

Answering these questions will help you decide on the length, scope, content, structure, development, style, and tone of your message.

All readers are motivated by their needs and interests. If you can see your message through your reader's eyes, your task will be enormously simplified.

Writing for a Diverse Audience

Analyzing the needs of your reader is a primary step in planning an effective piece of writing. When you write to multiple readers who have a similar knowledge of, and interest in, the subject, you can write to one representative person in the audience. But when the intended readers have different needs, interests, or roles, your job is not so simple. How can you effectively reach a diverse audience?

Begin by identifying the primary readers and the secondary readers. Primary readers are those who have the greatest "need to know." They are the ones who will generally have to act, or reach some decision, after reading your report; thus, they are the ones you should cater to. Secondary readers are those who, while interested, do not need the same level of detail. They are generally reading to become informed, not to act. Resist the urge to cater to the secondary audience, even if they are of higher rank.

The following devices will help both sets of readers:

Covering memos. Write different covering memos to each audience. Primary readers will need little information in this memo, though you can use it to point them to sections of special interest. Secondary readers will appreciate all the guidance you can give them. Provide them with additional background or with supplementary information. Steer them toward sections of particular interest and away from sections that are too detailed or technical. Make them feel comfortable with the subject. If necessary, use this memo to deal with politically sensitive matters as well.

Summaries. Start with a summary of the whole report. If the report is long, also include internal summaries, either at the beginning or at the end of each section, so that both sets of readers will stay on track. Even if you must lapse into technical language elsewhere, keep the language in these summaries easy to understand. Secondary readers may not need to read anything more than the summaries. (See "The Executive Summary" on pages 67–70.)

Headings. Since not everybody will want to read everything, use lots of headings and subheadings. These will enable readers to find relevant information and skip over irrelevant information.

Marginal notations. Unless a document is highly formal, individualize it by adding customized comments in the margins. Use colored ink, Post-it®notes, stars, or other symbols that will help readers.

Appendices. If you are including information of interest only to specialists, put it at the end of the report. The general reader will appreciate not having to wade through it, and the specialist will appreciate having it together in one place.

Finally, realize that sometimes in trying to please everyone with one report, you may please no one. If the needs of the audiences are so diverse that even the preceding suggestions will not help, write separate reports.

Organizing Your Thoughts

Once you have defined the purpose and scope of your document and have pulled together the information, you may be tempted to begin writing at once. Resist the urge. Instead, ask yourself how you should organize the information for maximum clarity and impact.

Avoid organizing the information the same way in which you thought it through. Most readers want the results of your thinking, not the thinking itself. Remember that there is a difference between thinking and communicating. Be ready to abandon traditional academic, scientific, or business patterns that require you to build to a conclusion. Most readers want to get important information at once.

Start by listing randomly all the ideas you want to include. (See "Deciding What to Say" on page 12.) Organizing from this list will help you see how the parts fit together. Experiment with various ways to organize the information. Be guided by two factors: (1) your reader's knowledge and interest and (2) your purpose and the information itself.

YOUR READER'S KNOWLEDGE AND INTEREST

Assess your reader's knowledge and interest in the subject. One of the following approaches may be appropriate for your document:

Use a *general-to-specific* approach (your main point followed by specifics) when your audience is familiar with your subject. Assume, for example, that management is well aware of four accidents that occurred in a manufacturing plant last year. You decide to recommend that greater safety precautions be taken (the main point of your memo). You could first recommend the actions you think should be taken. Then you could briefly discuss the accidents and explain how your recommendations would prevent recurrences (the specifics).

Use a *specific-to-general* approach if your reader has little knowledge of the subject. If, in the example above, management did not know much about the accidents, you would first discuss them before getting to your point—recommending actions to ensure safety. Be careful not to discuss the accidents in elaborate detail before getting to your main point, however. Even if you organize the document from specific-to-general, you should start with an opening sentence that addresses the main point.

Order your points from *most important to least important* whenever possible, and especially if your reader is busy or only mildly interested in the topic. This method of organizing will ensure that your reader will at least read the important information.

Order your points from *least important to most important* if you guess that your reader might be resistant to accepting your point of view or if you want to end powerfully. Most business readers want your best reasoning first; therefore, order your ideas from least to most important only if you are certain readers will stay with you to the end.

YOUR PURPOSE AND THE INFORMATION

In addition to analyzing your reader's knowledge and interest, also consider your purpose and the information you need to convey. One of the following standard modes of organization may be used in conjunction with the approaches mentioned above:

Use **chronological order** when the time or sequence of events is important. For example, if you are describing a new procedure to your staff, organize the steps in the order in which they should be done. If you are presenting the major events of the year for the annual report, go through them in sequence (January to December) or in reverse chronological order (from December to January).

Use **classification** to break a large topic into smaller components. If, for example, you are discussing the cost involved in changing over to new equipment, you would break down, or classify, the various costs (the equipment itself, service contracts, installation, training), and then discuss each category. In another case, you might classify the constraints your department faces in implementing a new procedure (poor timing, insufficient equipment, and untrained personnel).

Use **space or geographical orientation** when you want your reader to visualize the placement of objects or areas on a diagram or map. If you are describing the layout of a new warehouse, mentally walk your reader through it from one end to the other. If you are writing about shipping products to stores from the nearest warehouse, go from west to east or from north to south rather than discussing the sites randomly. Use visuals, floor plans, maps, or diagrams whenever possible.

Use **comparison or contrast** when you discuss two or more alternatives. If, for example, you are explaining several health plans available to employees, you would probably describe each plan separately and then compare them in terms of their advantages and disadvantages. But if you are considering three software packages for possible purchase, you might first set up a list of important criteria (the ability to manipulate data, compatibility, ease of use, cost, options for future upgrades) and then show how the different packages match up against these criteria. Setting up a chart can also help your reader sort out the information.

Use **problem–solution** when you want to suggest one, or several, ways to solve a problem. Begin by describing the problem, identifying its causes, and elaborating on its effects. Make a case for one or more solutions. If you present several solutions, use comparison (above) to help make your case.

Use **cause-to-effect** when you want (1) to discuss why something happened or didn't happen or (2) to predict what will happen as a result of some event or action. In the first situation, you might, for example, show that turnover in the advertising department (the effect) came about as the result of three factors (causes). Or, in the second situation, you might want to show the various outcomes (effects) of your company's expansion into Asia (the cause).

Only after you have analyzed your reader, your purpose, and the information will you be able to structure your document effectively. Experiment with various approaches; sometimes you may need to use a combination of approaches. The way you organize a document can make your writing easy or difficult to follow. It can also increase or decrease your reader's receptivity to your message.

Managing the Process of Writing

In our high-speed, high-tech culture we expect many tasks to take far less time than they do. Writing is one of them. But writing is a high-level conceptual skill and it does take time. Many mental activities are taking place at, or about, the same time: analyzing the audience, remembering and deciding on what information to present, organizing the information, putting it into comprehensible sentences, paying attention to the rules of good writing, making sure the words you have chosen will have the right effect on your reader. . . . The task can be monumental.

If you already have an efficient system for writing, continue using it. If you do not have a system, or if you want to streamline your own system, consider the following one. It breaks the writing task into several stages, thus allowing you to focus on completing one step at a time.

Professional writers often break the task down into the following steps:

Worrying and procrastinating
Deciding what to say
Organizing
Writing the draft
Getting distance from the draft
Revising the draft
Proofreading

Worrying and procrastinating can actually be productive. Do not scold yourself for delaying a project at its outset. Unless your writing is fairly routine, you usually need some time to warm up to your topic. Let your mind wander. Many of your best ideas will occur to you at odd moments during the day or night. Like many writers, you may excel at this phase of the process but lack momentum to proceed to the next phase. Try setting a strict time limit for this step. Then mentally let go of the project. Allow your subconscious to take over.

Deciding what to say will be easier if you first put down all your ideas about a topic—without evaluating or censoring them. Jot them down quickly and randomly. Put down every idea that comes to you—even if you know you will not include all the ideas in the final document. The mind often thinks by association; thus, putting down even tangential ideas may lead you to the next idea that *is* important. Then take a break so that your thoughts can "cook" or incubate. When you return (in a few minutes or hours) go through the list selecting those ideas that are essential to your message and to your reader. Cross out irrelevant ideas and add new ideas that have since come to mind. If you notice some holes in your thinking, fill them in.

Organizing requires that you experiment with various approaches until you find one that does justice to the content, one that is easy to follow, and one that will keep your reader's interest. Once you have listed all the information, find a way to easily move your ideas around. (Try writing each major idea on a small index card or Post-it® note. Then move these notes around.) Consider the progression of ideas from your reader's point of view. Then draft the document and see if your plan works. (See "Organizing Your Thoughts" on pages 8–11.)

Writing the draft should be a quick process. Take up your ideas one by one and put them into words, sentences, and paragraphs. Imagine you are talking to your reader. Keep moving. Try not to get bogged down. If you can't think of the "right" word, put down the "not-quite-right" word or leave a blank space. The draft will be rough. Do not perfect or overwork your thoughts at this stage. Simply get your thoughts down. Coming back to an imperfect draft is far better than coming back to a blank page or computer screen.

Getting distance from the draft will allow you to see your work more objectively. Horace, the early Roman poet, is said to have suggested that no document be published for eight years after being written. This cooling-off period would allow the author to decide if the piece of writing were still worth publishing. Though Horace's timetable is poorly adapted to today's fast-paced world, his basic point is sound. If you can get away from your draft for eight days, eight hours, or even eight minutes, when you come back to it, you will notice ideas that should be added, omitted, or clarified.

Revising the draft may take as much as half of your total writing time. In this phase, you'll test the ideas and structure of the document, rearrange ideas within paragraphs, rewrite awkward passages, choose words for precision and proper tone, and check grammar and punctuation. This polishing stage will ensure that the document is as professional as you are.

Proofreading the document (later in the day, or the next day) will allow you to find careless mistakes that might lessen your credibility. Enlist the aid of a few helpers. It is often difficult to find your own mistakes.

Some documents take longer to write than others. Some may be more troublesome, depending on the subject or audience. Do not adhere to this system, or any other system, slavishly. You may be drafting the document and choose to revise a poorly phrased sentence immediately. Or you may be revising the draft when you realize you have left out important facts. Every creative process requires flexibility. Do not let good ideas get away from you. But do find a systematic approach. Falling into a known system will help you override the inertia that can otherwise overtake you.

Overcoming Writer's Block

Every writer has suffered from writer's block—that painful inability to get one's thoughts on paper. This disability afflicts all kinds of writers: writers of fiction and nonfiction, the disciplined and the undisciplined, the veteran and the novice. Unlike other maladies, writer's block is not cured by taking two aspirin and going to bed. On the contrary, such treatment aggravates the condition since pressure mounts and panic increases as the task is delayed. Because each bout of writer's block may stem from a different cause, different treatments may be advisable.

COMMON CAUSES AND RECOMMENDED TREATMENTS

Lack of Preparation

Frequently your ideas won't flow because you haven't decided what you want to say. Figuring out what you want to say while trying to say it may seem efficient, but this approach is counter-productive. You'll end up not thinking coherently and not communicating clearly.

Treatment. Before you begin to write, you should be able to state your purpose and what you hope to achieve. Fill in the blanks in the following sentence *before* you write.

The purpose of this letter is to_____ so that my reader will _____.

If you aren't able to complete the sentence above, you'll first have to discover what you want to say. Often freewriting (writing quickly without laboring over your thoughts) will loosen you up and give you a sense of your purpose.

Ideally you'll be able to say something like this before you write: "My purpose is to inform my boss of the backlog in the publications department so that she will hire an additional editor." Once you know why you are writing, you'll need to continue the planning process. (See "Managing the Process of Writing" on pages 11–13.)

Misconceptions about Writing

You might think that once prepared you should be able to produce a nearly perfect product easily and swiftly.

Treatment. Writing is hard work. Although preparation will help, it will not eliminate the tedium of putting your thoughts into words. Even professional writers grope for their thoughts much the way one gropes for familiar objects in the dark.

Self-Consciousness

Because your writing will be reviewed and criticized by others, you may become obsessed by what others will think of you.

Treatment. Careful preparation will help you decide what to say and will give you confidence that what you put on paper will not make you look foolish. Others are probably not nearly so critical as you imagine. They will quickly read what you have written, giving you the benefit of the doubt as to what you say and how you say it. (We all know of exceptions, of course.)

Avoid leaving the project to the last minute, for you will rarely do your best writing under pressure. Instead, write and then let the document sit for a day or two. You'll be able to come back and make sure it is good.

Confusing Writing with Editing

You may become bogged down because you edit excessively as you compose. Switching back and forth between creative and censoring modes interferes with the flow of ideas, words, and sentences.

Treatment. Separate the writing phase from the editing phase. When drafting, write without interruption. If you cannot think of the right words, capture your idea in words that come to you quickly. Your goal should be to get your ideas down, lest they escape you. Suspend criticism until you have completed the draft. Then apply your best critical skills in evaluating and revising your writing.

Boredom

Working on a project often requires hours of intensive reading, research, and discussion. It is not uncommon to feel bored with a topic before you even begin writing.

Treatment. Like completing any project that you dread, you'll simply have to discipline yourself to get the job done. Set aside a certain time of the day to write, set deadlines for yourself, and focus on the finished product and its importance to you and the reader. Allow the pride of authorship to override your boredom.

ADDITIONAL AIDS

- Warm up to your subject by talking about it. Talk to a person or into a machine. Speaking is quicker and easier than writing. Hearing your own ideas may stimulate your thinking and get you in the mood to write.
- Start writing the section of the document that comes most easily, or, depending on your makeup, with the section that is most difficult. In either case, don't feel that you must write your ideas in the order in which they will finally appear.
- Avoid writing, if possible, when you are emotionally or mentally preoccupied.
- Find the time of day and the place that you do your best writing. Surroundings can influence your readiness to write—and your mood.
- Promise yourself a reward for your hard work.

3

Making Your Message Accessible

The Subject Line

Your aim in business writing should be to communicate as clearly and concisely as you can. It is no virtue to have your reader read to the middle or end of a memo and only there discover what it is about. You can prevent such a communication breakdown by supplying an informative, specific subject line.

The subject line on a business letter or memo serves the same purpose as the headline of a newspaper story: It engages the reader's interest. In writing the subject line, pull key words—specific action words—from the piece up to your headline. Make sure that the subject line is unambiguous and that it accurately represents what follows.

In routine memos, a topical heading such as "Agenda for October Meeting" or "Follow-up on Contract Talks" will suffice. In non-routine memos, however, the subject line should do more than simply identify a broad area. It can also give specific information about the subject, limit and focus the memo, and even motivate the reader to read on. Notice how the second subject line in each pair below improves upon the first:

Re: Expense Accounts
Re: Procedures for Submitting Expense Accounts

Re: Changing Our Discount Policy
Re: Increasing User Discounts by 15%

Re: New Software
Re: Bugs Found in New Software

When your reader can react to your subject line by asking, "What about it?" you haven't done your job. Be sure you answer the reader's question: "What about the new software?" "It has some bugs."

One exception is worth noting. If you anticipate that your reader will react negatively to a subject line, write a more general one. "Revised Vacation Policy" is less alarming than "Cut in Vacation Days."

Beginnings

The only requirements for beginnings are that they be clear and purposeful. Your reader wants to know at once *why* you are writing and *what* you are writing about. Thus, you should begin by stating these essential points:

- The purpose.
- The subject.

Depending on your purpose and your reader's familiarity with the subject, you may want to include some of these additional points:

- The context or background.
- The importance of the subject.
- An overview of the main points.
- The way the document is structured.
- Your conclusions and recommendations.

Not all these points need to be included, nor do they need to follow any particular order. In reading the three examples below, notice which points have been included and how they have been ordered:

Our recent merger requires that we adopt the personnel policies of our parent company. These policies are quite different from those we have been following. Please review the comparisons set out in the next few pages so that you will understand how the new policies will affect you.

❖   ❖   ❖

Seventy percent of contractors who have substantially renovated buildings in our state during the past five years have chosen electric heat over other heating sources. I recommend that you use electric heat when you renovate the Packard Building. This letter (1) describes all feasible sources of heat for the building, (2) explains why electric heat is best for your purposes, and (3) compares the cost of electric heat with other sources.

✦   ✦   ✦

We have been actively working toward eliminating theft in the stores in our franchise area. Several measures have already been taken. We have added cameras and increased the number of security personnel. Next Monday at 9:30 we will be meeting with you to discuss measures that can be taken by regular store personnel—salespeople, cashiers, custodians. Please read over the following suggestions and come to the meeting with ideas of your own.

Endings

When you come to the end of a document, both you and your reader need a sense of closure. You must settle the business at hand and leave your reader with a strong final impression. Depending on the purpose of your document, you may do one or more of the following:

- Reiterate important points.
- Draw conclusions.
- Recommend actions to be taken.
- Motivate action.
- Suggest next steps.
- Invite your reader's involvement.

The examples below round out and pull together earlier parts of the document:

After December 15, you will have to wait an entire year to switch from one plan to another. Thus, if you wish to make a change, you must complete and return the enclosed application before December 15.

Please call Mary Moffo in the Benefits Office (Ext. 3369) if you have any questions.

✦   ✦   ✦

Thus, leasing 10,000 square feet will provide you with the additional space you need. The first floor of the building at 300 Madison Street will be available for rental beginning September 1. It meets all your requirements and is in the price range you stipulated.

If you like, I can arrange for you to see this space. If you would like me to look for other rental space, I will be pleased to do so. I will be in town all week and look forward to hearing from you.

❖   ❖   ❖

I believe we should seek another vendor immediately, for we cannot afford to have our image suffer from the low-quality work done by XCel Company. I am in the process of meeting with other vendors. By the end of the week I'll provide you with a table comparing their services and prices.

Can we meet next Monday, after the weekly planning session, so that we can reach a decision?

Headings

Well-written headings serve important purposes. They enable readers to skim a piece of writing, get an overview of its contents, and focus on issues of interest. They enable you to highlight important points and break up long blocks of solid print.

Headings are not easy to write, for they must fulfill several requirements. Four major requirements are explained below.

Headings should show the relationship of ideas. By simply looking at a piece of writing, a reader should be able to tell which topics are of major, secondary, or minor importance. All topics at the same level of generalization should have headings that look the same; that is, their typography and placement should be identical. The typographic options available on most computer printers provide a wide range of design choices. Headings can be underlined, boldface, all capitals, or a different typeface. Higher-level headings should have more visual impact than lower-level headings.

Headings should be informative. Just as the headings in newspapers provide readers with information, so too should the headings in business documents. A heading should give as much information as possible. The heading "Bright Future for Product X," for example, can be made more specific: "Sales of Product X to Double by 2001." Broad headings like "Background" and "Conclusion" should be replaced with headings that summarize the background ("Regulation Has Limited Our Marketing Efforts") or state the conclusion ("Deregulation Will Open New Markets").

Headings should match the information in scope. Headings should fit the material that follows them; they should be neither too broad nor too narrow. If a heading reads "Homeowners Protest Ruling," the discussion that follows should be limited to only that point. If those who rent property are also discussed, the heading should be broadened: "Residents Protest Ruling." If only owners of vacation homes protest the ruling, the heading should be narrowed: "Owners of Vacation Homes Protest Ruling."

Headings should be parallel. Headings at the same level should be grammatically parallel. For example, if a section of a report discusses problems that lie ahead, the headings must be in the same grammatical form: "Patent Expiring," "Market Share Decreasing," "Labor Force Shrinking." (See "Parallelism" on pages 114–115.)

Notice how headings have been used in the sample letters and memos throughout this book. (See especially page 29 and pages 97–98.)

Graphic Devices

Readers choose documents primarily because of their interest in the subject and its importance to them. Beyond that, they choose short pieces over long ones and those that look easy to read over those that look tedious. Thus a writer today must pay attention to how a document looks, for if it is not visually inviting, it may not be read.

Computer programs offer wonderful choices. Become familiar with the array of graphic devices available to you. Try them out, but be careful not to overuse them, for a busy-looking letter or memo may distract your reader. Use graphic devices to highlight only important points.

A basic principle of graphic design states that anything different from what surrounds it calls attention to itself. Thus, if you underline and "bold" one word in a memo, your reader's eye will be drawn to that word. In deciding what to highlight, go through the document asking what portions the reader would underline. What would he or she consider most important? Then use some of the following graphic devices to make those portions stand out.

White space. Use plenty of white space (generous margins, breaks between paragraphs, indented lists) throughout the document—and especially to set off important points.

Boldface. Words or passages set in boldface (the first word in this paragraph is "bold") are attractive and eye-catching. One warning: Sometimes boldface does not reproduce well. If you are making multiple copies of a document, you may prefer to use a different device.

Underlining. This neat-looking device is dynamic—though it seems to have fallen out of use. Don't forget about it, but limit its use to passages no longer than one or two lines.

Capitals. Often overused by lazy typists, this device is best used only in short passages. Using all caps reduces reading speed by about half.

Bullets. These black dots (•) that precede listed items are used to set off major points that can be expressed briefly. They are widely used because they telegraph information quickly. (See "Bullets" on page 24.)

Typefaces and Type Style. Choosing a typeface or type style is a matter of personal preference, but some are easier to read than others. Compare the following:

This is a serif typeface. Notice the little horizontal lines (serifs) above and below the stem of the letter *i*. These lines make it easier for us to distinguish one letter from another.

This is a sans serif typeface. It is cleaner looking, but it is not as easy to read as a serif type because its letters have fewer distinguishing characteristics. Use sans serif for short passages or headings.

Italics, because they are slanted and lighter than regular type, also take longer to read. Save this type style for short passages of lesser importance.

Special Effects. Boxed or shaded items can attract your reader's attention, as can the use of color.

The layout of your document conveys a strong visual message to your reader. Use graphic devices to reinforce your verbal message. HIGHLIGHT ONLY IMPORTANT INFORMATION; otherwise the purpose for using these devices will be defeated—your reader will be distracted rather than engaged.

The bland format of the following report works against the reader's desire to read it. Compare it to its revision on page 23. Notice the use of graphic devices throughout the book.

January 15, 1996

Today I met with Charles LaRosa, CFO of Sea Products, Inc. The meeting was intended to be of an introductory/exploratory nature since Charles and I had never met. We discussed many issues in our short meeting.

Charles needs a cash management service so that he can keep track of daily balances, including those at other banks. He has looked at First Federal and County Bank's services but was eager to hear about our Multibank service. I tentatively scheduled a meeting for January 24 so that Eric and I can fully explain how the service works.

Charles mentioned three projects he'd like to fund through IRBs: $1.5 million to expand port facilities in Gloucester, $1 million to establish a warehouse in Essex, and $7 million to build a plant in Salisbury. Although First Federal has provided IRBs in the past, Charles said neither First Federal nor County Bank was interested in these deals. I turned down the $7 million plant but told him we'd fund the remaining $2.5 million, subject to agreeable pricing.

He also mentioned that Sea Products' union wants a guarantee for the company's annual $1 million payment to the pension fund. I explained how a stand-by letter of credit might guarantee this payment. I offered him a price of .050–.075%. He wants more information and a firm price.

Barbara Greyson
Barbara Greyson, AVP

January 15, 1996   <u>SEA PRODUCTS, INC.</u>
                                 Meeting with Charles LaRosa, CFO

Today I met with Charles to introduce myself as the new officer on the account and to get a sense of Sea Products' current banking needs. Discussion centered around cash management, IRBs and a stand-by letter of credit.

<u>Cash Management</u>

Charles needs a cash management service so that he can keep track of daily balances, including those at other banks. He has looked at First Federal and County Bank's services but was eager to hear about our Multibank service. I tentatively scheduled a meeting for January 24 so that Eric and I can fully explain how the service works.

<u>IRBs</u>

Charles mentioned three projects he'd like to fund through IRBs:
         $1.5 million to expand port facilities in Gloucester,
         $1 million to establish a warehouse in Essex,
         $7 million to build a plant in Salisbury.
Although First Federal has provided IRBs in the past, Charles said neither First Federal nor County Bank was interested in these deals. I turned down the $7 million plant but told him we'd fund the remaining $2.5 million, subject to agreeable pricing.

<u>Stand-by Letter of Credit</u>

He also mentioned that Sea Products' union wants a guarantee for the company's annual $1 million payment to the pension fund. I explained how a stand-by letter of credit might guarantee this payment. I offered him a price of .050–.075%. He wants more information and a firm price.

<u>Follow-Up Steps</u>

- Call Eric for 1/24 meeting.
- Propose price and terms for IRBs.
- Check price on letter of credit with Ned. Write proposal for this business.

                                Barbara Greyson
                                Barbara Greyson, AVP

Bullets

Bullets (black dots that precede listed items) are popular graphic devices. They help emphasize key ideas, and they help readers extract those ideas quickly.

Bullets should be used sparingly, for if you overuse them, they will lose their impact and confuse your readers. Readers may fail to notice important ideas if other less important ideas are also highlighted by bullets.

Newspapers have long used bullets. The following requirements and guidelines for using bullets are consistent with the method used by most major newspapers.

REQUIREMENTS OF BULLETED LISTS

Two requirements, based on the logic of outlining, apply to bullets: Bulleted items must (1) be at the same level of specificity and (2) be grammatically parallel—that is, they must be worded similarly.

In the following example, the four bulleted points are not at the same level of specificity:

The task force identified several reasons for excessive breakage in shipping.

Packers failed to do the following:
- Use heavy cartons.
- Pad the tubes adequately.
- Seal the cartons securely.
- Meet standards because of inadequate training.

The fourth item above is more general than the previous three points and might, in fact, be the cause for the first three failings. It should be eliminated from the list. It could be included in the lead-in ("Because of inadequate training, packers failed to. . . "), or it could appear as a separate sentence following the list ("These packing standards were not met because packers have not been adequately trained"). The list is grammatically parallel. Each bulleted point begins with the same kind of word, a verb in this case.

In the following list, the items are at the same level of specificity, but they are not grammatically parallel:

Each department head will be responsible for the following:
• Reducing overtime costs.
• An update of job descriptions.
• Provide training to new employees.

If all points began with an *-ing* word (*reducing, updating, providing*), the list would be grammatically parallel. (See "Parallelism" on pages 114–115.)

GUIDELINES FOR BULLETED POINTS

Because bullets are relatively new to business writing, no strict rules govern their usage. Some firms have style guides to ensure that everyone in the firm uses bullets the same way. If your firm has no such guidelines, follow these:

• Limit a sequence of bulleted points to just a few.
• Use bullets before phrases, sentences, or passages of only a few lines.
• Word each point succinctly.

Punctuation of bulleted points follows no set rules. In the examples above, and throughout this book, the style common to several major newspapers is used. Each point begins with a capital letter and ends with a period. Phrases and sentences are treated similarly. A colon follows the lead-in sentence.

An Easy-To-Read Style

Style in writing comprises many elements—organization, paragraph and sentence length and structure, and word choice. Style refers to the way your writing reads and sounds—the way you present your ideas.

An easy-to-read style allows readers to understand what you have written in one careful reading. They should be able to move along at their normal reading pace.

Though short words, short sentences, and short paragraphs will keep your readers from getting bogged down, your style may lack flow and rhythm; thus, you will also want to make sure that your ideas are well connected and that the rhythm resembles the rhythm used in speech.

Reading a piece of writing aloud (or, even better, having someone else read it aloud to you) will help you hear how it sounds. If it is hard to read aloud, it will be hard to read silently.

Compare the following passages. The ones to the left are harder to understand than the ones to the right.

The currency rates that are presently being used to calculate the revaluations made every month are not being compared to a designated independent source to determine whether they are accurate. Due to the fluctuating nature of currency rates, it is imperative that the rates used in the calculation be subject to a comparison to assure their accuracy.	Currency rates used in calculating the monthly revaluation are not being checked for accuracy against a reliable outside source. Because the rates fluctuate widely, such a comparison should be made.
Over the next several years, Citizens Air is planning to purchase and begin operating several fully modern aircraft (five Boeing 747s, two DC-10-30s, and three 200-seat airbuses—all to be delivered in 1998), which will allow the company to increase domestic service by 15% and to begin penetrating the burgeoning international market. Its international service will increase by 40%, as the new aircraft will be utilized on the traffic-intensive corridors of London, Paris, and Frankfurt. The increase in domestic service will be possible because of the new 747s.	Citizens Air is planning to expand its service over the next several years. It has ordered five Boeing 747s, two DC-10-30s, and three 200-seat airbuses for delivery in 1998. The 747s will be used to expand domestic service; the DC-10-30s and the airbuses will be used to service the international routes that Citizens has just been awarded. These routes include London, Paris, and Frankfurt. When the new aircraft are operating, Citizens' domestic service will increase 15%; its international service will increase 40%.

(Also see Chapter 5, "Editing for Language, Style, and Tone" on pages 40–59 for more suggestions on style.)

Strengthening a Weak Memo

Read and compare the memos on pages 28 and 29. The first memo is weak and uninteresting. The layout does not invite reading. The purpose of the memo is broadly stated; thus, the reader must read on to find out what exactly it is about. The writer takes his readers through his reasoning process, giving too much background and not enough details about the new program. The writer doesn't sound committed to the project, nor does he give helpful information.

The second memo invites reading. It is quick, clear, and direct. The writer makes specific suggestions. He seems knowledgeable and interested in the project.

Country Clothes, Ltd.

Interoffice Memorandum

To: Regional Managers   February 12,1996

From: *WPC*
Warren P. Chase, Vice President of Marketing

Subject: Change in Policy and Procedures

As you know, we have made several changes in procedures over the past year. These changes have dealt with efforts to improve the efficiency of our internal operations.

Now that certain improvements have been instituted, we must turn our attention to other matters. In particular, we must look at the markets we are serving.

For many years we have outfitted young adults aged 20 to 30 years old. These 20- and 30-year-olds have grown up, and, even though they are older, they want to dress casually. We want to continue selling to them; thus, we must begin placing an emphasis on casual clothes that are appropriate to those in the 35 to 65 age groups.

Please be advised that we will discuss this shift in emphasis at the quarterly meeting, Before then, begin thinking of ways you can begin this shift. Buyers will have to order different styles and sizes. Advertising and displays will have to be changed. Some personnel considerations also bear discussion.

Feel free to begin making changes that will benefit your region and bring all your ideas to the meeting next month.

Country Clothes, Ltd.   *Interoffice Memorandum*

To: Regional Managers   February 12, 1996

From: Warren P. Chase, Vice President of Marketing

Subject: Shift in Marketing Emphasis

In the past we have targeted our marketing efforts to young adults, those 20 to 30 years old. Over the next year, we will be shifting our emphasis to an older adult market—to those between 35 and 65.

RATIONALE. Until recently, young adults tended to dress more casually than those 35 and over; thus we catered to this younger market. Now, people of all ages dress casually, and we want to begin serving this broader population. Moreover, the mix of the population has changed. People aged 35 to 65 make up 25% of the population. This percentage will grow over the next decade and beyond.

IMPLEMENTATION. At our quarterly meeting we will discuss ways to implement a formal company-wide program; however, as you see opportunities to begin this shift, take advantage of them. Consider making some of the following changes, as appropriate, in your region:

Buying. Advise your buyers of our revised strategy so that they can begin filling our racks and shelves with products that will appeal to this age group.

Sales Force. In hiring new sales personnel, hire mature adults, as well as young adults. (Review Bulletin #6 on "Discrimination and Hiring Policies.")

Displays. In displaying merchandise, both inside the store and in windows, choose styles, colors, and fabrics that appeal to this group.

Advertising. Ask your advertising agencies or departments to focus their efforts on reaching this age group. Have them place ads in media that are popular with this group.

This changeover should be gradual. We do not want to lose younger adults, but we want older adults to feel that our stores serve their needs as well.

At our meeting in April, please be prepared to talk about what you have done, or plan to do, in your area. In the meantime, please share your immediate ideas with the other managers and me.

4

Shaping Paragraphs and Sentences

Paragraph Focus and Topic Sentences

A paragraph is a group of sentences that develops only one idea or one part of an extended idea. This idea, or topic, is usually encapsulated in a sentence called "the topic sentence." The topic sentence defines just what can be covered in a paragraph. Staying within the boundaries of that topic sentence will ensure that your paragraph remains focused.

The topic sentence may appear anywhere in the paragraph or not at all. By putting it near the beginning, you let your readers know immediately what the paragraph is about. In business writing, the topic sentence should most often be placed at the beginning of the paragraph. By putting it near the end, you build up to your main idea. By not putting in a topic sentence, you assume that the central idea of your paragraph is so clear that it need not be stated.

The following paragraph focuses on a single idea. The topic sentence, the first sentence, limits the items that can be discussed to very few:

> Your securities are safe with your broker. All securities held for you by your brokerage firm are insured by Securities Investor Protection Corporation, a congressionally-chartered company. Your brokerage firm may also take out additional insurance from a commercial insurance company. If your brokerage firm goes under, you will not lose the securities it holds for you.

Notice how the addition of a few more ideas destroys the focus and flow of the paragraph and weakens its impact:

Your securities are safe with your broker. The securities your broker holds are not in your name but in "street name." The brokerage firm assigns these shares to your account. All securities held for you by your brokerage firm are insured by Securities Investor Protection Corporation, a congressionally-chartered company. Your broker may also take out additional insurance from a commercial insurance company. If your brokerage firm goes under, you will not lose the securities it holds for you. If your securities are in your own safe-deposit box, they are not automatically insured against fire or theft. You must take out your own insurance.

The second and third sentences in the paragraph above add irrelevant details and distract the reader from the point of the paragraph. The last two sentences dealing with keeping securities in a safe-deposit box also depart from the central idea—safety in keeping securities with a broker. These last two sentences could remain in this paragraph if the topic sentence were broadened. It might read as follows: "Keeping securities with your broker might be safer than keeping them in a safe-deposit box."

The following paragraph focuses on a single idea. Notice how specific facts lead to the concluding statement, the topic sentence.

Next year Avondale will spend $150,000 more to dispose of its trash than it did two years ago. Last March skyrocketing disposal costs forced Glenbrook to raise the cost of a permit for bringing trash to a local transfer station from $1 to $125. Overall, the average cost of burning or burying garbage has tripled since 1993. As landfills close and incinerators fill to capacity, cities and towns are scrambling for places to dump their refuse. Residents of most communities are paying ever-higher prices to dispose of garbage in ever-fewer places.

The next paragraph contains no topic sentence as such, yet—except for one sentence that should be omitted—the paragraph holds together nicely:

The mall will be constructed on the site now occupied by the Plains Upholstery plant. It will consist of 250,000 square feet of retail space on two levels, 20,000 square feet of parking space, and 10,000 square feet of outdoor recreation space. Swartz Management is now trying to attract tenants to the mall. Construction will begin in August; the mall will be ready for occupancy next June.

The second-to-last sentence ("Swartz Management is. . . .") diverges from the main focus of the paragraph—construction plans for the new mall. When you are drafting a piece of writing, ideas may come to you so quickly that you do not want to take the time to sort them into neat, well-focused paragraphs. But when you come back to revise, make sure that each paragraph holds together as a unit and that your topic sentence helps define what the paragraph is about.

Paragraph Development

Some writers fail to appreciate the importance of substantiating their ideas with supporting facts or explanations. Their readers get interested in the subject only to be disappointed when no further information is provided. Other writers get so carried away with a subject that they go into too much detail. Their readers get bored or stop reading. Thus, when you write, you will have to decide how thoroughly to develop your ideas.

If an idea is important to your discussion, take the time to develop it adequately, but not excessively. The kind and amount of development will vary according to your purpose and your reader's level of knowledge and interest.

The following paragraph appeared in a brochure put out by a bank. Its purpose was to interest customers in taking out a home-improvement loan. The paragraph needs to be further developed:

> Home improvements enhance the appearance of a home, make it more comfortable, and add to its resale value. In general, the longer you live in your house, the more your home improvements will be worth in the future.

Adding specific examples to the paragraph above makes it more interesting and more convincing:

> Home improvements enhance the appearance of a home, make it more comfortable, and add to its resale value. In general, the longer you live in your house, the more your home improvements will be worth in the future. By modernizing a kitchen or bathroom, you can expect a return of from 80 to 125 percent on your initial investment upon resale. By making your house more energy-efficient, you can recoup from 60 to 75 percent on your investment, in addition to the money you will save on heating and cooling costs. By improving the exterior of your home—doors, windows, roofing, landscaping—you can get back from 50 to 75 percent of your investment.

If the paragraph were to go into much more detail, it might not hold the interest of the general reader.

(See "Paragraph Focus and Topic Sentences" on pages 30–32 for other examples of paragraphs that are adequately developed.)

Paragraph Length

Readers today are more used to reading short paragraphs than long ones. Indeed, many readers are put off by long paragraphs because they make a piece of writing look tedious. If a paragraph runs more than ten to twelve lines (about two inches), you should consider breaking it into two or more paragraphs, even if it develops a single idea.

The length of a paragraph depends on the information it conveys and on the length of the document. If you were writing a one-page memo briefly discussing several facts, you would write several short paragraphs, one for each fact. But if you were writing a long report in which you were explaining detailed concepts, your paragraphs could be longer. If you were writing a transitional paragraph, it might be only two or three sentences long. Occasionally, if you wanted an idea to stand out, you could write a single-sentence paragraph.

When a paragraph gets too long, look for logical points at which to divide it. Sometimes the breaking points are obvious; sometimes they are arbitrary. Where would you break the following paragraph?

> The request for a $400,000 increase for the budget for Phase I is justified. Construction costs will increase about $10,000 per unit because the majority of buyers want to upgrade the basic unit by purchasing options that were not figured into the initial budget. These options include brickfacing the fireplaces, installing better quality fixtures in bathrooms, and painting the interior of the garages. These add-ons would account for $300,000 of the additional funding. Approximately $75,000 would go toward additional labor costs, and the remaining $25,000 would be spent on administrative, legal, and miscellaneous expenses. These funds should be made available by the end of the month so that we can stay on schedule.

One can make a case for breaking the paragraph above after the second sentence or after the third. The last sentence could even appear as a separate paragraph if you wanted it to stand out.

In deciding where to break a paragraph, first look for logical points at which to break. Then see how each new paragraph holds together. Look at the information that precedes and follows the paragraph in question, and decide what information you want to emphasize (beginnings and endings of paragraphs are emphatic positions). Also look at the length of surrounding paragraphs, for variety in length is desirable. Parcel out the information into manageable units, each of which retains a focus while connecting well with what comes before and after.

Sentence Length and Rhythm

Vary the structure and length of your sentences so that the rhythm and pace of your writing does not become monotonous. In the following passage the ideas unfold too slowly. Sentences are similar not only in length but also in structure. The rhythm is choppy.

> The Haupt Corporation will close its plant in El Paso next fall. The closing will occur because of military cutbacks. The closing will put 1,000 people out of work. Military cutbacks will also cause the company to close a plant in Mobile. Next fall, 300 employees will be laid off and 500 will be reassigned.

The following passages demonstrates a different problem:

> Next fall, because of military cutbacks, the Haupt Corporation will close its plants in El Paso where 1,000 people will be put out of work, and in Mobile, where 300 employees will be laid off and 500 reassigned.

This version is overly compressed. The reader must collect and retain a lot of information.

The ideal, of course, is to allow ideas to flow at just the right rate. Readers literally need to blink to lubricate their eyes. Mixing the length and structure of sentences results in a pleasant, easy-to-read rhythm.

> The Haupt Corporation will close its plant in El Paso next fall, putting 1,000 people out of work. Another plant in Mobile will also be closed, forcing about 300 employees to be laid off and 500 reassigned. According to management, both plant closings have been caused by military cutbacks.

Reading your writing aloud (or having someone read it aloud to you) will give you a sense of the rhythm. If your sentences fall into too steady a singsong pattern, you will want to revise them. Similarly, if you find yourself gasping for breath, while the period sits at some distance ahead, you will want to revise the passage. By varying the structure and length of your sentences, you can keep your reader from being lulled to sleep or from becoming exhausted.

Sentences Joined by *And*

And is frequently used to join two sentences. It is used correctly when it joins two related ideas of equal importance:

> The president is in Tokyo, and the treasurer is in Paris.
> Volume has increased, and profits have rebounded.

And is used incorrectly, however, when it joins two ideas that bear a more complex relationship than that signified by *and*. (*And* simply signals an additional thought.) If one idea is causal or conditional, or if a time sequence is suggested, *and* should not be used. Note the following revisions:

CAUSAL:	Profits increased 15% last quarter, and we'll get a bonus.
	Because profits increased 15% last quarter, we'll get a bonus.
	Routing slips were lost, and our shipments will be delayed.
	The loss of the routing slips will delay our shipments.
CONDITIONAL:	Lower your overhead, and your profits will increase.
	If you lower your overhead, profits will increase.
	Send me the spreadsheet, and I'll check the figures.
	If you send me the spreadsheet, I'll check the figures.
TIME SEQUENCE:	All bills have been paid, and we know we stayed within budget.
	Now that all bills have been paid, we know that we stayed within budget.
	He arrived in Atlanta and realized he had lost the report.
	When he arrived in Atlanta, he realized he had lost the report.

In rereading your draft, circle every *and*. Question its use. Does *and* obscure a more complex relationship between ideas?

Hard-To-Read Sentences

Business readers should be able to read a sentence once and understand it. Short sentences are generally easier to follow than long ones, but even long sentences can be easy to read if they are structured carefully. To keep long sentences from becoming unwieldy, (1) retain normal word order, (2) keep the subject and verb close to one another, or (3) set off material that comes between the subject and verb.

1. Retain normal word order.

Subject. . . verb. . . object is the most frequently used order for words in a sentence: **S   V   O**
He bought a house.

In the following sentence, three objects come first, followed by the verb, and finally the subject:

Careless circling of the number of units ordered, incorrect or missing code numbers, and misspelled customer names were the most common mistakes.

The sentence reads more easily, and more quickly, if the subject . . . verb. . . object pattern is retained:

The most common errors were (1) careless circling of the number of units ordered, (2) incorrect or missing code numbers, and (3) misspelled customer names.

The following sentence should also be revised to retain normal word order:

A raise he has asked for and a raise he will get.
He has asked for a raise and he will get one.

2. Keep the subject and verb close to one another.

In the following sentence, the subject comes at the very beginning, the verb at the very end:

<u>Production increases</u> resulting from the growing use of digital technology, electronic switching, and fiber optics, coupled with a projected 6% gain in telephones in service, <u>will aid</u> profits.

In the revision, the sentence is broken into two sentences. The subjects and verbs are closer to one another:

<u>An increase</u> in production and a projected 6% gain in telephones in service <u>will aid</u> profits. <u>The increase</u> in production <u>will result</u> from the growing use of digital technology, electronic switching, and fiber optics.

In the next sentence, 19 words come between the subject and verb:

<u>Big Tin Company</u>, despite its diversification into aluminum recycling and resource recovery, businesses that have done well over the last two years, <u>has continued</u> to lose market share to competition.

One way to revise the sentence is to put the verb immediately after the subject:

<u>Big Tin Company</u> <u>has continued</u> to lose market share to competition, despite its diversification into aluminum recycling and resource recovery—businesses that have done well over the last two years.

3. Set off material that comes between the subject and the verb.

The sentence above about the Big Tin Company can also be revised by setting off the intervening material with dashes. Dashes are visually emphatic; thus, the reader can see the interrupting material that comes between the subject and verb:

<u>Big Tin Company</u>—despite its diversification into aluminum recycling and resource recovery, businesses that have done well over the last two years— <u>has continued</u> to lose market share to competition.

If you tend to write sentences like the hard-to-read ones above, take pity on your readers. Revise the sentences into manageable, easy-to-read units.

Connecting Sentences and Paragraphs

Your writing will be quick and easy to read if sentences and paragraphs flow gracefully. The order of ideas within sentences and paragraphs obviously affects the flow. A number of explicit transitional devices can also provide the connections that will make your writing coherent.

CONNECTING SENTENCES

When you speak, you connect ideas quite naturally by repeating *key words* or by using *synonyms* and *pronouns.* The same transitional devices can help you connect sentences when you write.

Notice how these devices (underlined in the paragraph below) help join ideas:

> Last month we <u>surveyed customers</u> in the Long Branch store to see if they liked the electronic <u>scanning system</u> at our checkout counters. The results of <u>this survey</u> showed that 83% of our <u>customers</u> liked <u>the system</u> (1) because <u>they</u> felt confident that <u>they</u> were charged the correct amount and (2) because <u>they</u> felt that <u>the system</u> allowed for quicker checkouts. On the basis of <u>this study,</u> we will expand the use of <u>scanners</u> to our other stores in the state.

You may also use some of the following *transitional words and expressions* to link your thoughts. The choice of the correct transition depends, of course, on the relationship of the two ideas:

ADDITION:	and, in addition, also, too, furthermore, moreover
SEQUENCE:	first, second, then, next, finally, now, later, before, after
COMPARISON:	similarly, likewise, in comparison
CONTRAST:	but, however, though, nevertheless, yet, on the other hand
ILLUSTRATION:	for example, in particular, for instance, that is, specifically
RESULT:	therefore, because, accordingly, consequently, thus, hence, as a result
SUMMARY:	to sum up, in summary, in conclusion, finally

A final device, repeating the same sentence structure in several sentences (parallelism), can help your ideas flow rhythmically. (See "Parallelism" on page 114–115.)

The transitional expressions and parallelism in the following paragraph make it easy to read and follow:

> We will not meet our target date for implementing the new system <u>because</u> departments have failed to coordinate with one another <u>and because</u> two vendors have failed to ship equipment on time. We can, <u>however,</u> be operational by March 15 if we take the <u>following</u> steps immediately: <u>First, we should encourage department heads to discuss</u> the situation <u>and to appoint</u> a liaison to improve interdepartmental interaction. <u>Second, we should contact</u>

<u>the vendors</u> who are supplying equipment <u>to make sure</u> new delivery dates are firm. <u>Third, we should budget funds</u> to train all personnel in the new operation <u>so that</u> no further delays will occur when we convert to the new system. <u>As a result</u> of taking <u>these steps</u> we can be up and running before our busy season.

CONNECTING PARAGRAPHS

The kinds of transitional devices that work well between sentences also work well between paragraphs. They quickly, and unobtrusively, link paragraphs. In some cases, however, you may need a more explicit transition—a complete sentence or paragraph.

In writing a transitional sentence or paragraph, you'll usually summarize what has gone before and anticipate what is to come. If you have explained the advantages of a plan in one paragraph, the next paragraph might begin this way: "Although the plan has several advantages, it also has some disadvantages."

When you take great leaps in thought, you might even need to write a short transitional paragraph. In the example below, the writer has spent several paragraphs discussing a timesaving method to collect samples. She now shifts to a discussion of the longer-than-normal testing phase.

> Although the new equipment will allow us to collect samples in half the time it now takes, testing these samples will still be a time-consuming task. In fact, because new procedures for testing will become necessary, testing may take up to 20 percent longer to perform.

Besides verbal signals, you can use visual signals—headings and subheadings. These signposts will let your reader know that you have come to the next stage of your discussion. The heading alone may suffice, or you may want to add a short transitional sentence as well.

Transitional words, sentences, and paragraphs help your readers know where you are going. If your direction is obvious, you do not need to use a transitional device. (Too many transitions can be as annoying as too few.) But if your readers stand a chance of getting lost, signal the turns you are taking in your thought.

5

Editing for Language, Style, and Tone

Editing Is a Must

Only 0.8 percent of the human race is capable of writing something that is instantly understandable.

H. L. Mencken

Unless you are part of that minuscule minority (0.8%), editing is a must. Editing means reviewing what you have written for its effect on the reader, not simply changing a word here, a comma there. Think of editing as the final quality-control inspection before the product leaves your desk.

Whenever possible, try not to edit your draft soon after you've written it. Getting away from it for a time may help you see its strengths and weaknesses. (If you've ever come upon something you wrote a year or two ago, you can appreciate how important the passage of time is to changing your perceptions about a piece of writing.)

When you edit, put yourself in the reader's place. Ask the questions your reader might ask: What does this word mean? Why didn't you tell me that fact sooner? Why are you boring me with all those details? What do you want? How much will it cost? By adopting your reader's point of view, you may be more objective than you might otherwise be. (Also see "Seeing the Message Through Your Reader's Eyes" on page 6.)

Then use the checklist below, or one of your own making, to ensure that you look at, and catch, every weakness in a draft. The checklist has been organized into five broad areas. Try to make five quick passes through your draft, focusing on one area at a time, rather than looking for everything in a single pass. This methodical approach may slow you down, but editing is an exacting procedure. In some cases, revising a document may account for at least half of the total time spent on the writing project.

A CHECKLIST FOR EDITING

Purpose

Will the reader know—early in the piece—why you are writing?

Content

Keeping the intended reader in mind, is the information complete? Is it accurate?

Should any information be added, deleted, modified?

Are the points adequately, but not excessively, developed?

Organization and Layout

Would the information be clearer, or have greater impact, if it were reorganized?

Does each idea proceed logically from the previous idea?

Is the layout functional and appealing? Does it highlight important points?

Paragraph Structure

Does each paragraph make one major point?

Is each major point explicitly stated?

Can long paragraphs be divided or short ones combined?

Style and Tone

Is the language specific, natural, and appropriate to the reader?

Can unnecessary words or phrases be deleted?

Are sentences varied in structure and in length?

Is the piece direct, clear, easy to read?

Does it flow smoothly?

Is the tone consistent with your purpose?

Mechanics

Is the grammar correct throughout?

Is the punctuation correct throughout?

Are all words spelled correctly?

Avoiding Language That Is Outdated or Faddish

If you want your writing to sound crisp and contemporary, you will have to avoid using words and expressions that while once considered standard, are now considered outdated. If you want your writing to sound businesslike, you'll also have to avoid using faddish or trendy words that may fall out of use as quickly as they came into use. Thousands of words lie between these two extremes. Using them will help you achieve a style that is up-to-date and professional.

OUTDATED WORDS AND PHRASES

Business language borrowed from an earlier generation can make your writing sound artificial or pedantic. Every letter will sound like a form letter, and you will sound bored, or, even worse, boring. Thinking up substitute phrases is easy if you put your mind to it.

Please be advised that *or* Hereby	*Both these expressions can be eliminated.*
We acknowledge receipt of	We have received *or* Thank you for
As per your request	As you requested *or* You asked me to
Please do not hesitate to contact me if you have any questions.	Give me a call if I can help in any way. *or* Please call me if I can be of further assistance.
Attached herewith	I have attached
Enclosed please find	I am enclosing

FAD WORDS

New words come into use when they provide a meaning that existing words do not capture. Many new words are born of new technology, events, or life-styles ("byte," "lift-off," "triple by-pass," "cyberspace," "roller-blading"). Once coined, these words can help you express yourself more clearly, succinctly, and colorfully. But if you use words that have not yet become current—words that do not yet appear in the latest edition of a good dictionary—you can confuse readers. If they are unable to understand the meaning of a word, they will supply their own meaning, or they will ignore the idea entirely.

A sampling of memos from various firms yielded these curiosities:

Will you <u>bottom-line</u> that for me?
Listed below are <u>possible actionable areas</u>.
I don't see any <u>windows</u> for the next two weeks.
Now that Tom is finished using the equipment, can we <u>repurpose</u> it?
<u>Calendar</u> these important dates.

What are the dangers of using such words in correspondence? First, readers may not understand precisely what you mean. Second, readers may need to slow down while they figure out what you mean. Third, your style may be inconsistent. (See "Consistency in Your Choice of Words" on pages 45–46.) Fourth, you may come across sounding less than professional.

In reviewing your draft, look at the words you have chosen. When you come upon words—either very old or very new—that you would never use in polite conversation, rid your writing of them, too.

Using Words That Are Familiar and Concrete

If you are serious about making your writing clear, you will have to question the words you use and eliminate those that your reader might misunderstand or not understand. You should not talk down to your readers, but neither should you try to impress them with your extensive vocabulary. Most readers are unimpressed with such displays. If you can get your message across simply and clearly, you may, instead, impress them with your efficient handling of the business at hand.

USE FAMILIAR WORDS

If you use words familiar to your readers, they will be able to read at their normal pace. But if you use specialized terms (jargon) or unusual words, your readers will have to slow down or puzzle over them.

Every field has its own jargon. Bankers speak of *T-bills;* environmental scientists speak of *ecosystems;* graphic artists speak of *kerning.*

When writing or editing, constantly remind yourself of who your readers are. If they will understand the specialized terms, use them. If they might not, define the terms, or use other more familiar words. Thus, the banker might want to recommend Treasury bills to a customer. The environmental scientist might explain the specialized term: "In an ecosystem, a community consisting of all the organisms living in a place,. . . " The graphic artist would tell the neophyte that *kerning* means adjusting the spacing between letters.

Since it is easy to slip into jargon without realizing it, let someone outside your field read your draft. Ask that person to circle every word or phrase that is confusing. Then make those ideas clear to your reader.

Besides avoiding specialized vocabulary, avoid using uncommon words. Some readers, however well-educated, may have limited vocabularies. Other readers, even if they have extensive vocabularies, do not want to expend much mental energy reading business documents. They want your ideas in the simplest, most lucid language possible.

The length of a word is not necessarily at issue here. Many long words are familiar (*cooperation, circumstance, conversationalist*), while many short ones are not (*cant, carp, cull*). But if two words, one long and one short, have the same meaning and are equally familiar, choose the shorter one. Your style will be less high-sounding and easier to read.

Compare the following pairs of sentences:

Once he becomes acclimated to the department, he will be more amicable.
Once he becomes used to the department, he will be more friendly.

The hiring embargo will be a bane to the department.
The hiring freeze will be a burden to the department.

The first sentence in each pair tries too hard. The sentences are stilted. The second sentence in each pair above uses familiar words. The sentences read well.

Write to inform, not to show off or to test your reader's vocabulary.

USE CONCRETE WORDS

Words can be concrete (that is, specific) or abstract (that is, general or vague). "Considerable savings" is abstract. "A savings of $1,000 per month" is concrete. The phrase "as soon as possible" sounds specific but is vague compared to "by noon tomorrow."

In speaking of its Certificates of Deposit, a bank brochure states that they are written "for large amounts and relatively short maturities." How are readers to know what is meant by the abstract words *large* and *short?*

Abstract words, like abstract art, are open to the reader's interpretation. One person reading the bank brochure might consider putting $200,000 into a certificate as a week-long resting place for some funds, while another may consider tucking away $200 toward a trip to Europe in two years.

As ideas become more specific, they become more informative. The second sentence in each pair below is more concrete than the first:

Security must be strengthened.
Passes must be checked at each entrance to the facility.

We will soon offer extended banking hours.
Beginning September 1, the bank will be open from 9:00 A.M. to 5:00 P.M. each weekday and from 9:00 A.M. to 1:00 P.M. on Saturdays.

Sometimes you will want to make broad statements. Then you will use general words (*wealthy, assets, office supplies*) instead of concrete words (*a millionaire, real-estate holdings, six double-sided disks*). Whenever possible, be specific. You will save your reader from misinterpreting, or having to question, vague generalities.

Writers who are unsure of their message often choose vague or unfamiliar words. By not pinning down ideas, these writers may feel they are not really accountable for them. When you sit down to write, make sure you know what you want to say. Then say it as simply and precisely as you can.

Consistency in Your Choice of Words

Linguists commonly categorize language as formal, standard, or informal. Achieving a consistent style requires that you choose words from the same general category.

In formal prose, words like *inquisitive, loquacious, to censure* are common. In standard prose, the everyday synonyms—*curious, talkative, to criticize*—would be used. In very informal prose, the slang or colloquial equivalents—*nosy, gabby, to pick on*—might be used.

Formal English is rarely called for in the business world. It is usually reserved for academic or literary writing. Its vocabulary often sounds pretentious. It requires greater effort to read than standard English. Standard English is the language used by most educated writers most of the time. It tends to be more concrete than formal English and thus is suited to the action-oriented world of business. It communicates clearly without calling attention to itself. Informal English, including slang, is relaxed and casual. It may be appropriate if you know your reader well and if your subject is not weighty.

REVISING FOR CONSISTENCY

In the following excerpt, notice the inconsistency in the level of words used:

> When senior management and <u>the undersigned</u> last met with Robert Troy, he asked that we consider granting his company a loan for $10 million so that it could begin expanding into the profitable southern markets. In making our decision we <u>perused</u> the company's financial statements for the past five years and also <u>touched base</u> with the company's accountant to <u>ascertain</u> the intended pay-back period. Since everything <u>checked out</u>, we called Mr. Troy and <u>rendered</u> our approval of the loan. Extension of the loan <u>warrants</u> quick action, especially since <u>it's in the wind</u> that he has also contacted other banks.

The passage should be revised for consistency:

> When senior management and <u>I</u> met with Robert Troy, he asked that we consider granting his company a loan for $10 million so that it could begin expanding into the profitable southern markets. In making our decision we <u>studied</u> the company's financial statements for the past five years and also <u>spoke with</u> the company's accountant to <u>determine</u> the intended pay-back period. Since everything <u>was in good order,</u> we called Mr. Troy and <u>told him</u> we had approved the loan. Extension of the loan <u>demands</u> quick action since it has been <u>rumored</u> that he has also contacted other banks.

Before you write, decide on the appropriate level of language. As you edit, look for words that diverge from that level. Revise them so that your language will be consistent.

(Also see "Avoiding Language That Is Outdated or Faddish" on pages 42–43.)

A Style for the Times

Perhaps no change in business writing in the last decade has been so dramatic as the change in style. The principles of good writing have changed little. Writing must still be clear, cogent, and coherent. Paragraphs must still be unified and adequately developed. Sentences must still be constructed according to the rules of syntax, and grammar and punctuation must still be correct. But style, once indirect, has become direct; once ponderous, has become brisk; once stiff, has become relaxed.

The style of our writing reflects the style of our work lives and of our personal lives. The efficiency brought by state-of-the-art technology has affected the way we do business and the way we communicate. The openness in the way we relate to others has affected the way we communicate with them. The changeover can be seen in the way a piece of writing looks, in the way it is structured, in its length, language, and tone.

Business writing no longer presents the reader with solid masses of print. Long blocks of prose are broken up into more manageable units. Headings and graphic devices (boldface, underlining, bulleted lists) make it easy to skim.

Few letters begin at the beginning and take their readers to the end. Instead, they begin where they used to end—with conclusions and recommendations. The conclusions and recommendations are then explained or justified. Because of this change in structure, the approach, or style, has become direct, vigorous.

Some firms require that memos be one page or shorter. Some consultants who used to supply a hefty report (to justify their fee, I'm told), now supply a slim summary report. Executive summaries (short synopses of reports) now accompany the report. The length of paragraphs and sentences has also decreased.

Formal language has been replaced by the brisk everyday language of business. Tone, while still courteous, is less artificial, more sincere.

These changes respond to the needs of today's readers—decision makers down the hall who need to become informed and act quickly, or clients and customers who want to understand a letter in one reading.

Achieving an Effective Style

Your writing style can be termed "effective" if it is (1) appropriate to the context and purpose of a document and (2) appropriate to the audience.

Your writing style can vary just as your mode of dress can vary. Sometimes you'll want to be proper and well dressed; at other times you'll want to be relaxed and casual. When writing a proposal to the executive committee, your style will be more formal than when you're writing a memo to a colleague asking for a simple favor. One style will simply be more "dressed up" than the other.

The range of acceptable styles in business writing is broad. Two extremes should be avoided: a stiff, overly formal style and a breezy, overly colloquial style. Your style should be professional but not stiff, cordial but not cute. Your wardrobe, or repertoire of styles, should suit the occasions for which you write.

Notice the differences in style in the next three documents. The style of each is appropriate to its purpose and audience.

The letter on page 49 is informal. The language is colloquial; the tone is conversational.

The letter on page 50 is straightforward and businesslike. It uses standard English. The tone is professional.

The memo on page 51 is more formal. The tone is serious sounding, as is dictated by the situation.

12 McFarlin Rd.
Chelmsford, MA   01824
March 29, 1994

Al Scalera, Store Manager
Purity, Inc.
Boston Rd.
Chelmsford, MA 01824

Dear Mr. Scalera:

Just a quick note to compliment one of your employees.

I was recently standing in the Express Checkout Line, about 4th or 5th in line.
There was a bit of a computer problem with the register and the line was
growing longer. Your employee, Karen R. (sorry I don't know her last name),
jumped in and opened another register. But it wasn't what she did that
deserves praise, it's the way she did it.

As I saw her approaching the new register, I prepared myself for the jousting
match that usually occurs when a cashier announces, "Register #11 is open."
Often the person who has been waiting the least amount of time zips into the
new line first. Then, everyone juggles back and forth and gets pretty
frustrated.

What Karen did was look right at the person who'd been waiting the longest
and said, "I believe you're next." Right on! At that moment, with a simple
reminder, everyone in line actually acted like an adult. People were making
sure that everyone was treated fairly. At first I stayed in line 12 but then
decided to move over to line 11. The woman who was ahead of me turned to
me and suggested that I go ahead of her because she realized I'd been waiting
longer. Amazing!

If Karen used this method on her own, she deserves high praise. If it came
about as a result of management training or store policy, then you all deserve
praise. It made a big difference in the attitude people had when they were
leaving the store. I hope all cashiers in your store follow this terrific example.

Even for "responsible" adults, simple but positive guidance about fairness
makes everyone happier.   Good Job!!!

Sincerely,

Steve Kinnal
Steve Kinnal

Fall 1995

Dear Prospective Management Student:

Thank you for your interest in the Radcliffe Seminars Graduate Program in Management. I am enclosing a 1994-95 catalogue, which provides detailed information on the program. Although the catalogue will answer many of your questions, I want to emphasize a few aspects of the Radcliffe Seminars that our women and men students tell us provide the greatest benefits:

Stimulating Seminar Format.   This is the 44th year Radcliffe will offer graduate-level education in a seminar format and the 14th year of the Graduate Program in Management. With a maximum of twenty-five students enrolled in any seminar, each class provides an intimate and challenging learning environment.

Excellent Faculty.   Faculty members at the Seminars are recognized leaders in their fields. They are both practitioners and academics who are committed to teaching excellence. They are skilled at creating stimulating interactions among students and between students and faculty. The Radcliffe Seminars Program is small enough to allow students to have extensive contact with and counseling from administrators and faculty.

Varied and Flexible Curriculum.   The breadth and depth of the Seminars' offerings are shown in the catalogue. Students are encouraged to follow a learning path appropriate for their individual needs. It is possible to enroll in a single seminar or a few seminars of particular interest, or to earn a Radcliffe College Graduate Certificate in Management. Since students come from both the business and non-profit sectors of the economy, courses appropriate to both areas are offered.

Your selection of an academic program is important. I want you to have the information you need to make the choice that is best for you. If you wish to discuss the Graduate Program in Management, please call me at 495-8600. We can either meet or speak by telephone. Faculty members are also available to discuss particular seminars.

I commend you for your interest in continuing your education and hope that you will find Radcliffe appropriate for your needs. Please let me know how I can help.

Sincerely,

Phyllis Strimling

Phyllis Strimling, Ed.M.
Coordinator
Graduate Program in Management

U.S. DEPARTMENT OF LABOR

SECRETARY OF LABOR
WASHINGTON, D.C.

FEB 22 1994

MEMORANDUM FOR ALL POLITICAL APPOINTEES IN
THE DEPARTMENT OF LABOR

FROM: ROBERT B. REICH

SUBJECT: Election Year Conduct

As the 1994 elections approach, it is important that all
Department of Labor employees conduct themselves in compliance
with the highest degree of integrity. The conduct of political
appointees in the Department will be under particular scrutiny.
Actions that would otherwise be seen as a legitimate and
responsible discharge of official responsibilities may, in
certain contexts, be perceived as improper involvement in
partisan political activities.

It is my expectation that all political appointees in the
Department will carry out their duties in a manner consistent
with all laws and regulations. It is especially important that
no employee of the Department use his or her official authority
or influence for the purpose of interfering with or affecting the
result of an election.

The Office of the Solicitor will be providing written
guidance and conducting training during the early part of this
year on the Hatch Act and other laws that govern your
participation in political activities. It is mandatory that you
attend this training. As you probably know, there have been
extensive changes to the Hatch Act that became effective earlier
in February. While a number of these changes permit increased
participation of employees in political activity during their
non-duty hours, other significant restrictions remain. The
Solicitor's Office will also be available for individual
counseling and advice in these areas. You are encouraged to call
Robert Shapiro, Associate Solicitor for Legislation and Legal
Counsel, at 219-8201, or David Apol, Counsel for Ethics, at
219-8065.

In sum, I expect that every political appointee will become
familiar with the applicable legal rules and carry out their
responsibilities in a manner which avoids even the appearance of
impropriety.

Tightening Your Style

I have written you a long letter because I have not had time to write a short one.
                                                BLAISE PASCAL

This quotation encapsulates an ironic truth. But the time you spend tightening your writing will be time well spent. Writers who are brief are perceived to be more decisive and confident than those who are verbose.

If you compress your message, you will endear yourself to most readers. A short document is more likely to be read than a longer one, and it is often easier to understand and remember.

The most obvious way to be brief is to eliminate information. Omit unessential background or details. Make sure every bit of information contributes to your message. Do not feel compelled to tell everything you know about a subject. Focus on the points your reader needs.

Once you have eliminated unessential information, go through each sentence getting rid of unnecessary words. Professional editors usually look for certain kinds of words or grammatical structures that force writing to become wordy. If you want your style to be brief and vigorous, become aware of the places to look for wordiness:

WHO AND *WHICH* CLAUSES

The use of *who* and *which* may force you to use more words than necessary:

> The travel office, *which* is located in the basement of Building 39, is open daily from 9:00 to 5:00.
> The travel office, located in the basement of Building 39, is open daily from 9:00 to 5:00.

> Daniel Stoddard, *who* is our dean of Academic Affairs, will call you.
> Daniel Stoddard, dean of Academic Affairs, will call you.

PREPOSITIONAL PHRASES

Commonly used prepositions include *across, after, as, at, before, between, by, for, from, in, on, over, through, to, under, until, with.* Prepositions are important function words, for they connect one idea to another, but if they are overused, they can cause sentences to become stringy:

> *In* the event *of* a price increase, we will renegotiate the contract we have *with* you.

If prices increase, we will renegotiate our contract.

The increase *in* investments *by* foreign nations is *of* concern *to* many economists.
Increased investment by foreign nations concerns many economists.

Be careful not to string together too many words just to avoid using a prepositional phrase, however. Clarity is more important than brevity.

The manager plans to support company budget-planning activities.
The manager plans to support the budget-planning activities of the company.

Many common expressions containing prepositions can be tightened:

in regard to = about	at a later date = later
along the lines of = like	at the present time = now
as soon as = when	by means of = by
due to the fact that = because	for the purpose of = for

REDUNDANCIES

Some banks offer "free gifts." Some insecticides "kill bugs dead." Develop an eye and an ear for detecting redundancies or repetitious expressions:

advance planning	refer back	consensus of opinion
final outcome	desirable benefits	basic fundamentals
new innovation	necessary requisite	end results
past history	large in size	future projections

THE VERB *TO BE*

Be, am, is, are, was, were, been, being are forms of the verb *to be.* Besides forcing wordiness, the verb *to be* is weak. (Notice below how prepositions sometimes attach themselves to the verb *to be.*)

The company *is* engaged in the processing of liquefied gas.
The company processes liquefied gas.

It *was* our advice that he find another job.
We advised him to find another job.

THERE IS AND *THERE ARE*

There is and *There are* should be eliminated from the beginnings of sentences if they steal the important opening position from other more important words:

> *There is* a possibility that performance reviews may be delayed.
> Performance reviews may be delayed.

> *There are* many reasons why we should delay the announcement.
> We should delay the announcement for many reasons.

NOUNS THAT COULD BE VERBS

Many nouns (typically those ending in *-tion, -sion, -ance, -ence, -ment, -ing*) can be replaced by their verb forms. (Notice how prepositions attach themselves to some nouns.)

> The committee took into considera*tion* the adop*tion* of the proposal.
> The committee considered adopting the proposal.

> When we held the meet*ing*, the vice-president made the deci*sion* that the committee should take ac*tion* immediately.
> When we met, the vice-president decided that the committee should act immediately.

WEAK VERBS THAT COULD BE REPLACED BY STRONGER VERBS

Several weak verbs (*make, take, give, have, bring, hold*) derive meaning only if they couple with a noun (especially those nouns ending with the suffixes mentioned above). Instead of using these weak verbs, change the accompanying noun to its verb form, or think of a more precise verb:

make a decision = decide	*make* a recommendation = recommend
take action = act	*take* into consideration = consider
give a response to = respond	*give* a promotion to = promote
have a tendency to = tend	*have* an ability to = can
bring to an end = end	*bring* to a resolution = resolve
hold a meeting = meet	*hold* a conference = confer

Active and Passive Verbs

Passive verbs have lessened the impact of the following well-known sayings and quotations:

> My heart was left by me in San Francisco.
> Only one life is had by me to be given to my country.
> "Cheese" should be said.
> Frankly, my dear, a damn isn't given by me.

Passive verbs can distort or have the same dulling effect on your writing. Whenever possible, use active verbs.

In an active sentence, the one who performs an action (the doer) precedes the verb:

> The clerk filed the applications.
> Gold Coast Properties earned money for the first time this quarter.

In a passive sentence, the doer appears at the end of the sentence, or not at all:

> The applications were filed by the clerk.
> The applications were filed.
> Money was earned for the first time this quarter by Gold Coast Properties.

Because the normal word order (subject-verb-object) is reversed in passive sentences, they are sometimes hard to follow. Because the doer of an action is sometimes omitted, the sentence may be vague or ambiguous. Passive sentences are longer and less vigorous than active sentences.

Passive verbs consist of the verb *to be* in any of its forms *(be, am, is, are, was, were, been, being)* plus the past participle, or third form of the verb *(sing, sang, sung)*. It's easy to make a passive sentence active. Simply begin the sentence with the subject, the "who" or "what" of the sentence. If you have omitted a doer, supply one when you revise the sentence:

Passive:	Budgetary limits *were set* by Congress.
Active:	Congress set budgetary limits.
Passive:	The new contract *was fought*.
Active:	The union fought the new contract.

Some writers use passive verbs because they are hesitant to use "I." In using passive verbs they also avoid taking responsibility for an action and may, as a result, lessen their credibility:

Passive: *It is recommended* that we accelerate our payments.
Active: I recommend that we accelerate our payments.

While active verbs are preferable to passive verbs, passive verbs do have a few legitimate uses. They may be used as follows:

- *When the doer of an action is unknown or unimportant—that is, when* **what** *was done is more important than* **who** *did it.*

  Kelly was promoted to senior vice-president.
  A cure was found ten years after the virus was identified.

- *When a statement needs to be softened or made impersonal.*

  The policy was disregarded.
  Performance goals were not reached.

- *When a smooth transition from the previous sentence will be achieved.*

  Ming Tang was familiar with all relevant export regulations. These regulations had been questioned earlier in the meeting by several committee members.
  The samples arrived on the noon plane. They were immediately sent to the laboratory, where Dr. Ryan was waiting.

Using *I*

Although the highly impersonal style that dominated business and government writing has all but vanished, you may still feel uncomfortable using *I*. Yet using *I* ensures clarity and directness, and it adds warmth to a piece of writing.

Use *we* when you are presenting the viewpoint of your firm, but use *I* when you are presenting your own views. Your sentences will sound natural, and you'll avoid slipping into passive verbs and awkward constructions:

Passive: It is recommended that we expand our service.
Active: I recommend that we expand our service.

Awkward: The report was written by the undersigned.
Natural: I wrote the report.

After you have drafted a piece of writing, review it to make sure that you haven't overused *I*. You do not want your writing to sound boastful or egocentric. If you fear that you are overusing *I,* try one of these tactics:

- *Move* I *from the beginning of a sentence to the middle:*

   I have been appointed to head the committee and I will be inviting members
      to speak at these meetings.
   As chairman of the committee, I will be inviting members to speak at these
      meetings.

- *Refocus a sentence away from yourself and onto the reader:*

   I will send you a list of suggested topics for these talks.
   You will receive a list of suggested topics for these talks.

- *Make a request instead of a statement:*

   I want you to get back to me by next Friday.
   Please get back to me by next Friday.

Tone

When you speak, those listening to you will pick up your tone of voice immediately. They may characterize it as "harsh," "sarcastic," "warm," "condescending," or "sincere," for example. When you write, your readers will also pick up on your tone and will characterize it similarly. Because readers react, and possibly overreact, to the tone of your writing, make sure the tone you convey is the one you intend. Print is permanent.

Though tone is evoked primarily by the words you use, it is also communicated by the amount and kinds of information you present and by the way you structure your message. In reading the following passages, notice that although the ideas are nearly identical, the tone differs significantly.

Passage 1

As a result of someone's carelessness with an ID card, outsiders penetrated our security twice last week and thereby obtained highly confidential materials. Because of this lack of care, we now face the problem of having to issue new ID cards to all holders of blue cards.

If you have a blue card, call Human Resources immediately to set up an appointment to get a new one. Once you have it, be sure to follow the rules regarding its use and be more careful in the future. Lost cards seriously threaten our security, and replacing them is expensive.

Passage 2

If you hold a blue ID card, please call Human Resources (Ext. 8998) this week to make an appointment to get a new one. Last week unauthorized persons obtained copies of confidential information after gaining entrance to what we thought was our highly secure computer area. Therefore, we are issuing new cards and tightening security.

The new ID cards will be specially coded so that only authorized personnel will be able to enter our high-security areas. When you pick up your new card, its use will be explained.

We rely on you to safeguard your card. Since we pride ourselves on our state-of-the-art systems, we must keep them secure at all times.

If the writer of the first passage truly intended to make all the readers (not merely the offenders) feel chastised, he or she certainly succeeded. One asks which memo is more likely to gain the cooperation and foster the goodwill of the employees. When you write, make sure that your tone doesn't work against your getting what you want.

Softening a Negative Message

When you write a negative message, you will want to make sure that it is clear but not unnecessarily harsh. Some of the distinctions below are subtle, indeed, but they may help you come across gracefully and diplomatically. The second sentence in each pair of sentences below is preferable to the first.

State what you can do instead of what you cannot do. Your readers may be more receptive to your ideas if you phrase them positively.

We cannot set up a meeting before May 15.
We can set up a meeting any time after May 15.

We will not process your order until you send payment.
We will process your order as soon as we receive payment.

Replace words that carry strong negative connotations. Some words, like *problems, mixed up, wrong,* and *lazy,* carry negative connotations. If you get rid of these words (unless you are purposely using them for emphasis), your tone will be more positive.

If you have any problems, please call me.
If you have any questions, please call me.

You sent in the wrong form.
We received Form A but need Form B to complete the transaction.

Depersonalize negative statements. Often you can temper your tone by shifting emphasis away from the person's action to the situation, or by shifting the point of view from *you* to *we.*

Your desk is always messy.
Because visitors see your desk when they enter the reception area, please try
    to keep it neat.

You will not be entitled to interest because you sent in your deposit after the
    10th of the month.
Unfortunately we can pay interest only on deposits made by the 10th of the
    month.

Using passive verbs (normally to be avoided) can also make statements impersonal:

You did not send in your application before the deadline.
Your application was received after the deadline.

6

The Politics of Business Writing

Office Politics and Interoffice Correspondence

A simple memo can cause tongues to wag, ears to burn, eyebrows to raise, and noses to be out of joint. It might even cause heads to roll. The interoffice memo is a powerful document.

Some offices are more political than others, but all operate according to certain unspoken rules. While the political environment and the rules of etiquette differ from company to company, the following general warnings may help you save your neck.

Know when not to write. Highly sensitive or highly personal messages are often better communicated "off the record." Information that is confidential or critical, bombastic or sarcastic should probably not be written either.

Send your memo to the right person. Send your memo to the person responsible for an activity or function. Never go over anyone's head. If you get no results, courtesy demands that you tell the person that you plan to take the matter up with someone in higher authority.

Ask "who" should sign a memo. Occasionally, even though you have written a memo, your boss might want to sign it. If you guess this might be the case, simply ask "Would you like to sign this memo, or should I?"

Send copies to the right people. Send a copy to anyone affected by, or interested in, the subject, anyone in a direct line of authority between you and the addressee, and anyone you have mentioned in your memo. Avoid sending copies to curry favor or to put someone on the spot.

Avoid turf battles. Concern yourself with issues that fall within your area of responsibility. If you are writing about an issue that involves others, or that others might see as their bailiwick, acknowledge their involvement, compliment them for their contributions, or invite them to collaborate in writing the memo.

Avoid surprising your reader. Prepare your reader for news that might be surprising, especially if the news will not be greeted with enthusiasm. Call ahead to say "You'll be getting a memo later today explaining why we have had to cut your budget," or attach a short covering note that softens the blow.

Give important information to important people first. If you are disseminating important information, consider sending it a couple of days ahead to important people or to those who would be embarrassed if they did not know about it before others. Not everyone reads mail when it arrives.

Ghostwriting

Until you've made it to the very top of the organization, you may be asked to write for someone else's signature. Conversely, as your responsibilities grow, you may ask others to write for your signature. Understanding the realities of the ghostwriting process may help you and your partner focus on the project and its successful completion.

Delegating the task. In order to write effectively, every writer needs to be well informed about the subject and the audience. If you are considering delegating a writing project, ask yourself who in your department understands the situation sufficiently to take on the task. Delegating work just to get it off your desk might be self-defeating, for you may end up having to complete the task yourself, usually after feeling disappointed with the writer's effort. If you do delegate the task, involve the writer in the situation and work closely with him or her—especially if that person has little experience writing.

Taking on the task. If you are the one asked to write a document for someone else's signature, consider it a learning opportunity. Throw yourself into the project, become informed, and ask copious questions. Don't try to write the whole document (if it is long) at once. Instead, draft sections and get feedback from the person who asked you to write.

Setting realistic expectations. No two people think, or write, the same way. Personalities differ and so do the ways we express ourselves. Thus the person who assigns a project should not expect the ghostwriter to duplicate his or her style. The ghostwriter should, in turn, expect changes to be made, even though the draft represents his or her best effort.

Clarifying the task. The two parties should discuss the project so that they are both clear as to its purpose, scope, and content. While one would hope that the person assigning the task knows what he or she wants, this is not always the case. Thus, the writer needs to ask questions before writing—and sometimes while writing—to ensure that the final product will be effective. Misconceptions about the task can lead to unnecessary work and to bad feelings.

Making the style authentic. The style will be authentic only if the one signing the document adds some personal touches to it. The ghostwriter may try to determine a few characteristics of the other person's style but should not become preoccupied with mimicking it. Even when the writer provides a well-written draft, it is the signer's prerogative to make changes as desired. After all, the final product will bear his or her signature.

Editing Someone Else's Writing

No passion in the world, no love or hate, is equal to the passion to change someone else's draft.

H. G. WELLS

Wells recognized the fervor that overcomes a person when editing someone else's writing. (Rarely does the same intensity carry over to the editing of one's own writing.) Few writers respond well to editors who make copious and thoughtless comments. Editing someone else's writing calls for objectivity, maturity, and tact. Few interactions demand more diplomacy.

A writer has put time and effort into preparing a piece of writing. In giving it over for editing, the writer is putting his or her ego on the line. As an editor, you should, therefore, realize that your remarks, however well meaning, may make the writer feel threatened. You are, after all, criticizing that person's work. Make sure that you are focusing on the written product and not on your feelings about the writer. Be balanced. Be specific. Be constructive. And be gentle.

Force yourself to read the draft in its entirety. Sit on your hands (literally) or make sure you have no pen or pencil in your hand. Give the draft a chance before you begin reworking it. When you have read it through, ask what overall impression the intended reader will have. What are the strong points? What are the weak points? How could the document be improved?

Only after you have carefully considered your comments should you begin writing them down. And do use pencil, not ink, so that you can modify your comments if necessary.

YOUR ROLE AND RESPONSIBILITIES

Your role as an editor is to sharpen the message and its impact by making as few changes as possible. This role requires that you look at what has been written from the intended reader's perspective, making changes or suggestions that will improve the document for that reader. You should make no change unless you can give a good reason for it. Finally, you should resist the urge to change something simply because you would have done it, or said it, differently. In short, you'll have to focus on the document and its effectiveness for the reader, not on your preferences.

In reviewing a piece of writing, look at issues like clarity, coherence, tone, and correctness. Pose questions like these:

Is the information accurate?
Are the points adequately, but not excessively, developed?
What questions will the reader ask? Should these questions be answered?
Is the document well organized and visually appealing?
Are paragraphs and sentences easy to read?
Are the language and tone appropriate?
Are grammar, spelling, and punctuation correct?

Use good judgment in responding to what has been written. Do not rob the writer of self-confidence. If a piece of writing is good, return it with a kind remark ("Great job," "Nice work"). Be careful not to over-edit, impose your style, or nitpick. If you do, the writer may not do the best possible job the next time around, knowing that you'll change everything anyway.

If the piece needs substantial editing, talk to the writer. Suggest changes you believe would improve the document and explain why they are necessary. If a writer needs help with his or her writing, provide some instruction, rather than scolding the person for the inadequacies.

Your role as editor is important, for you can look at a piece of writing objectively—something that is difficult, or impossible, for a writer to do.

(Also see "Editing is a Must" on pages 40–41 and "Ghostwriting" on pages 61–62.)

Language and Sexual Bias

Gender and gender bias have become political issues in many arenas. For centuries, masculine pronouns (*he, his, him, himself*) were used to refer to both sexes. A sentence like "Everyone has been issued his own identification card," was grammatically and politically correct. Business letters that began with the salutation "Dear Sir" were also correct.

As society and values change, however, so too does the language. The changes that have taken place in recent times are particularly noticeable in the workplace. Women now comprise nearly half of the work force. Women now hold jobs once held by men, and men now hold jobs that were once held by women. Gender-based stereotypes have broken down.

Occupational titles have become gender-neutral. Airline stewards and stewardesses are now referred to as flight attendants. Mailmen and mailwomen are now referred to as letter carriers. Firemen and firewomen are now called firefighters. "Men Working" signs have been reissued. They now read "Road Work." What once seemed extreme is now becoming commonplace.

No matter what your personal views are, when writing for business you must consider your reader's reaction to the language you use. You cannot afford to offend a reader, nor do you wish to be labeled "out of touch," or "politically incorrect."

If you refer to women differently from men, or if you use masculine pronouns instead of masculine and feminine pronouns, you may imply an attitude that could be objectionable to your readers, male and female alike.

The following tactics can prevent your excluding or offending a reader.

ADDRESS BOTH SEXES THE SAME WAY

If you are writing to a general audience, avoid using "Dear Sir" or "Gentlemen." Instead, use the title or role designation of the person to whom you are writing: "Dear Owner," "Dear Members," "Dear Customers." Using "Dear Sir or Madam" is acceptable, though it sounds a bit stuffy.

If you use a man's first and last name, use a woman's first and last name. If you use Mr., use Ms. or Mrs. If you do not use Mr., do not use Ms. or Mrs. If you use titles for men, use comparable titles for women.

Do not give out personal information (marital status, age, physical or personal characteristics) about people of either sex unless the information is relevant.

ELIMINATE MASCULINE PRONOUNS

If you are referring to people in general or to unspecified individuals, avoid using just masculine pronouns. Our language provides many alternatives:

Use Plural Nouns and Pronouns

> Each supervisor should inform his staff of the new policy.
> Supervisors should inform their staffs of the new policy.

Eliminate the Pronoun

> The boss who does everything himself will soon be overworked.
> The boss who tries to do everything will soon be overworked.

Shift to You

> Any employee wishing to change the beneficiary on his insurance policy should consult the Benefits Office.
> If you wish to change the beneficiary on your insurance policy, please contact the Benefits Office.

Whenever the reader can be addressed directly, *you* is preferred. *Caution:* Be careful not to shift back and forth between *you* and *he* and *she*. (See "Shifts in Person" on pages 115–116.)

Use Both Masculine and Feminine Pronouns

> A writer should insure that his style is authentic.
> A writer should insure that his or her style is authentic.

Caution: If this form is overused, it can be distracting. Even more awkward is the use of *s/he* or *he/she*. Used occasionally, *he* or *she* and *him* or *her* go unnoticed. Use this option when the alternatives mentioned above fail to capture your meaning.

In time, language will adapt to the current social and political realities. One or more of these forms—or some new ones—will replace the traditional forms. Meanwhile, these new usages may seem a bit strange, but lest a writer offend a reader, he or she should adopt them.

7

Writing for Special Purposes

The Executive Summary[*]

An executive summary is a short (usually a page or less) synopsis of a report. For some readers, the summary previews the report; for others, it replaces the full report. It should be comprehensive, yet concise.

STRUCTURE

Executive summaries take different forms depending on the nature of the report and on the practices of a company. Whatever the form, the opening sets the context and scope of the report. It reminds readers why the report was written or why it is significant.

In general, the structure of the executive summary reflects the structure of the report. For example, a traditional research report first sets the context, then explains the method of investigation, and finally presents the major findings, conclusions, and recommendations. An action-oriented report takes a more direct approach. It presents conclusions and recommendations immediately after the opening. Then it justifies them. (See pages 69 and 70 for examples of executive summaries that would precede these two types of reports.)

[*]This chapter is based on an article that appeared in the November 1983 issue of *ReWriting™*. The article was co-authored by Maryann V. Piotrowski and JoAnne Yates.

TIPS FOR WRITING

It's usually far easier to write the summary after you've written the report. Go through the report lifting out important information, findings, conclusions, and recommendations. Avoid including excessive background and detail.

One manager who had trouble summarizing a lengthy report discovered a helpful technique. He imagined that he and his boss got on the elevator on the 35th floor and rode down to the lobby. His boss remarked, "I just got your report on the new sales incentive plan. What's it all about?" The manager would—in the time it takes an elevator to descend 35 floors—give his boss the rationale, findings, and recommendations of the report.

Depending on how tall your building is—or how fast or slow the elevators are—you may want to try this technique to help you frame your summary.

EXECUTIVE SUMMARY

Expenses for air travel in 1995 totaled $2.3 million, a 20% increase over 1994. These expenses increased because more trips were made by a greater number of employees. We have examined travel records for these two years to determine if the expenses in 1995 were justified and to explore ways to further economize.

Methodology

We analyzed travel expenses by department and by region for both years. We noted which employees had traveled in each of the years and the reasons for their trips. We asked these employees to rate their trips in terms of value to the company and to project their travel needs for 1996.

Findings and Conclusions

Our research revealed the following:

- Two groups accounted for 80% of the increased travel:
    - Region 6 (West Coast) made 40% more trips (25% of these trips were to Asia) in conjunction with the joint venture.
    - The sales department made 12% more trips, all to conferences and trade shows, to achieve the 1995 corporate goal of broader exposure.

- Travelers felt that 90% of the trips taken in 1995 were necessary.

- Staff project that the joint venture and goals for the coming year will require the same amount of travel in 1996.

Based on the above, we have concluded the following:

- Increased travel in 1995 was justified.

- Travel in 1996 will not decrease significantly, given the joint venture and our goals for the coming year.

Recommendations

We recommend the following measures to cut down on travel:

- Encouraging employees to seek out the lowest possible fare.

- Setting up meetings via video conferencing.

- Scheduling trips to accomplish two or more purposes.

EXECUTIVE SUMMARY

Our inability to meet demand for the new Model QT terminals has created long shipping delays for customers. Though production will be increased when the Thompson plant begins shipping terminals in May, we may lose some important clients before then. Consequently, we recommend two short-term measures to ease the shortage.

Recommendations for Easing Shortage of QT Terminals

<u>Substitute Model PT for internal orders.</u> Three hundred Model QTs are on order by internal users. While we do not want to accelerate delivery to outside customers at the expense of our own efficiency, most of the QTs on order internally can be replaced by the Model PT. Where the PT is not suitable, shipment of the QT will be delayed for six months or more.

<u>Route QT parts directly to North Carolina for assembly.</u> Now all QT parts are routed from St. Louis to our warehouse in Delaware. By routing the parts directly to North Carolina, we can gain two weeks.

Clear Instructions

At one time or another you may have tried to follow instructions that forced you to throw your hands up in despair. Though seemingly a simple task, writing clear instructions demands careful thought and execution. Every step must be delineated, every doubt clarified, every risk defined. Whether a set of instructions is a formal document that will be included in a procedures manual or an informal note explaining how to get to the new plant, it should be simple and clear.

If you want to perfect the art of writing clear instructions, study the way recipes are written, for they incorporate several sound practices: They list everything needed to perform the task, give steps in proper sequence, describe the actions to be taken, use familiar words, and help cooks know when the intended results have been achieved. The writers of cookbooks realize that they have to step outside their own area of expertise to see a situation from the point of view of a novice.

Follow these ten steps to write good instructions:

1. ***Prepare your reader for the task.*** Start by defining the task and listing the equipment or materials necessary to perform it. If relevant, include other preliminary remarks that set up the process and describe its purpose or importance.

2. ***Use familiar terms.*** Remember that the person who needs instructions is unlikely to understand specialized vocabulary. A term like "sysgened configuration" tossed into a basic set of computer instructions should be avoided or, if used, should be defined in language everyone can comprehend.

3. ***Adhere strictly to chronological order.*** Be sure that the instructions give the steps in the sequence in which they should be performed. The next two sentences in a set of instructions should obviously be reversed: "Freeze the solution for several hours, or until firm. Before freezing it, make sure that the solution is blended well and that the color is uniform."

4. ***Give all necessary warnings.*** Explain conditions under which an operation should not be performed: "CAUTION: Do not operate this equipment during electrical storms."

5. *Relate the unknown to the known.* Compare the new task to one that is familiar to the reader: "Grasp the first chopstick like a pencil."

6. *Reassure the reader.* Insert occasional phrases that tell the reader he or she is proceeding correctly: "If you have completed this step properly, the green light will flash when you push the red button."

7. *Explain reasons for performing a step.* Tell your reader why a step is being taken if the explanation will help that person understand the process or complete the step accurately: "Maintain the activity for 20 minutes so that the full aerobic effect will be achieved."

8. *Use an easy-to-follow format.* Number the steps so that the reader will be able to focus on one step at a time and find the next step easily.

9. *Include drawings or diagrams.* Use a visual aid if it will explain something more clearly than words. Ensure that the artwork is simple and properly labeled.

10. *Try out the instructions.* Have someone follow the instructions so that you can discover where they are confusing or unclear. Revise the troublesome sections and test your instructions again.

The instructions on pages 73–75 tell the reader how to use the IBM Personal Computer's Disk Operating System (DOS) DISKCOPY command. These instructions may also be used on IBM-Compatible personal computers.

These instructions were written by Philip L. McCarron, an engineer and freelance technical writer from Boston.

Using the DOS DISKCOPY Command

Why Copy a Floppy?

When you purchase new software, one of the first things you should do is make a copy of the original floppy diskette. *WHY?* Because floppy diskettes are easily damaged. They're thin, they tend to be brittle, and their contents are susceptible to destruction by such common things as heat, magnetic force, and direct sunlight.

You can easily duplicate the entire contents of one floppy diskette onto another by using DOS's DISKCOPY command.

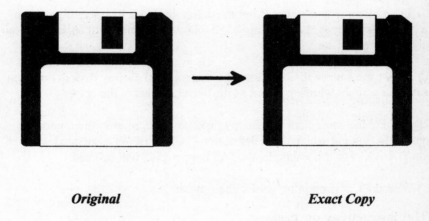

Original   *Exact Copy*

Figure 1 -- The DISKCOPY Command

How To Diskcopy A Floppy

Note: The original diskette (the one being copied) is referred to as the *source* diskette. The diskette which will become the exact copy is called the *target* diskette.

When using the DISKCOPY command, you **must** use the same type and size disks for both the source and target disks. For example, if the source diskette is a 3-1/2" 1.44-megabyte disk, the target diskette must also be a 3-1/2", 1.44-meg disk. The same applies to a 5-1/4" diskette.

CAUTION: The **DISKCOPY** command formats the target diskette before copying to it. Any data previously stored on the target diskette will be detroyed.

1.) Turn on your computer. After the computer loads its operating system (a process known as "booting up"), the following prompt will appear on your monitor screen: **C:>**

2.) Insert the *source* diskette into the appropriate floppy disk drive. You may hear a slight whirring sound as the diskette spins in the drive.

(If your PC has more than one floppy diskette drive, refer to the owner's manual to find out which drive delineator--"A" or "B"--is associated with which drive.) For this example, the "A" floppy drive will be used.

3.) With the C:> prompt on your screen, **type:**

> **DISKCOPY A: A:**
> **Press the ENTER key, and follow the instructions on the screen.**

4.) The light on the disk drive will illuminate, indicating drive activity. After a short while, the light will go out and the following message will appear:

INSERT TARGET DISK IN DRIVE A:
PRESS ANY KEY TO CONTINUE

5.) Remove the *source* diskette from drive "A," and insert the *target* diskette in its place. Press the ENTER key.

6.) The diskette will again whir and spin as it is being written to. The light on the disk drive will also illuminate. When the copy is complete, the following message will appear:

COPY ANOTHER DISKETTE (Y/N)?

If you have another diskette to copy, type "Y" and press the ENTER key. Continue by following the instructions on the screen.

If you have no other diskettes to copy, type "N" and press the ENTER key. You will be returned to the original system "C:>" prompt.

The *target* diskette in drive "A" is now an exact duplicate of the original *source* diskette and can be used to install your new software on your PC. Store the original diskette in a safe, cool, dust-free location away from direct sunlight and magnetic fields.

Goodwill Letters

"Goodwill" is the attitude a business conveys to its customers, vendors, and employees. Though we should strive to attain a friendly, yet professional, tone in all our correspondence, certain letters and memos can give us an opportunity to underscore to our readers the importance of our business relationship.

These unsolicited letters—congratulatory letters, thank you notes, apologies—let clients or colleagues know that they are important. And the trust that is built up over time really does become an asset a company can be proud of.

Sincerity is the key element in these letters. They should not sound like form letters; thus in writing them, avoid using trite business cliches. Pretend you are speaking to the recipient. Be warm, specific, and genuine.

Letters of Congratulations

Congratulatory letters always bring a smile to their reader's face. Critical statements are often openly broadcast, but compliments or recognition of accomplishments are less often voiced. Thus, taking a moment to acknowledge someone else's success can lift that person's spirits—and possibly the spirits of co-workers as well.

The memo on the next page is heartfelt and sincere.

INTER-OFFICE MEMORANDUM

December 15, 1995

TO: Peter Fowler, Foreman

FROM: Rafael Tejeda

SUBJECT: A Much-Deserved Promotion

~~~~~~

CONGRATULATIONS!

Word of your promotion reached me yesterday. I'm pleased that your hard work has been rewarded. The efficiencies you've introduced to the line have made a difference. Production has increased and the number of defective parts has decreased. The work crew even smile now and then. Nice job!

Thank-You Notes

The most important thing about a thank-you note is the fact that you've taken the time to write it. People scarcely remember what you say in the note, but they do remember that you've sent it. You needn't be clever, but you should be sincere.

In writing your note, consider these suggestions:

- Say "thank you" and indicate what you are saying "thanks" for.
- Mention how you, or others, benefited—overall and specifically.
- If appropriate, look forward to another opportunity to interact with the person.

A thank-you note should be short. Try double-spacing it or using small stationery if it looks lost on the page.

Thank-you notes, like the one on page 79, take a few minutes to write, but they go a long way toward making people feel good about themselves and about you.

United Way
of Pelham
P.O. Box 44
Pelham, NY 10803
(914) 738-0016

December 9, 1994

Charlotte Rose Babad
440 Fowler Avenue
Pelham Manor, NY 10803

Dear Charlotte Rose,

Thank you for your splendid willingness to help with our recent United Way of Pelham phone-athon.

In our three nights of calling, we generated pledges totaling $11,587—including $860 from new contributors—an amount we can be very proud of!

Twenty-two callers reached 259 donors; thus, each caller raised an average of $526.68 and each donor gave an average of $44.74. We could not have received this support without your efforts.

On behalf of the United Way of Pelham Board, let me again say "thanks" and offer you best wishes for a happy holiday season.

Gratefully,

Alex Hood
Phone-athon Chairman

Letters of Apology

Despite your best efforts—or those of your company—things don't always go right. In these cases, a company must decide if it is to its advantage to apologize or to simply let the matter go unmentioned. More and more, companies are taking responsibility for their actions and, by apologizing, are regaining the respect and goodwill of their clients.

Sometimes an apologetic sentence in your next letter can suffice. At other times, a specific letter of apology is preferable. When writing such letters, try to do the following:

- Send your letter quickly—as soon after the event as possible.
- Start with an apology.
- Explain what happened—or didn't happen—and why.
- Assure your readers that their business or patronage is important to you.

The letter on page 81 was handed out to subway riders the morning after train service was interrupted. Though the letter is long, riders were interested in every detail. The Washington Metropolitan Transit Authority received massive positive response to this letter from its clients and from local press.

Washington Metropolitan Area Transit Authority

600 Fifth Street, NW Washington, DC 20001-2693

(202) 962-1234

May 13, 1993

An Apology to Metrorail Passengers:

I would like to extend a formal apology to all Metrorail patrons who were inconvenienced by the disruptions in Tuesday morning's service. At approximately 8:30 a.m., a tragic incident occurred at the Judiciary Square Station requiring Metrorail officials to take actions that caused major gaps in service on the Red Line. In an apparent suicide attempt, a young woman walked into the tunnel between Union Station and Judiciary Square and, in spite of the operator's immediate response, was struck by the train.

It was imperative that power to the affected tracks be cut off immediately in order to permit the evacuation of the injured person and the safe exit of passengers from the train. Further safety concerns and constraints inherent in track design dictated the choice of Union Station and Dupont Circle as the terminal stations to be used on the Red Line for the time needed by emergency personnel to complete their work at Judiciary Square.

We share the public's heartfelt regret that an incident like this should ever occur. Unfortunately, albeit rarely, such things do happen, requiring measures to be taken immediately that will facilitate the handling of the incident, and ensure the least disruption to service. In this instance, the event took place at the busiest time on the busiest sector of our rail system, greatly increasing its impact on our passengers.

During morning rush hours, approximately 20,000 passengers per hour are served by the Red Line. The confusion that ensued when most of those passengers got off trains at Union and Dupont Circle Stations was inevitable. No station is equipped to handle such large numbers of exiting passengers. In an attempt to clear the platform and mezzanine areas as quickly as possible, and in contrast to normal morning operating procedures, most of the escalators at the Dupont Circle Station were deliberately set to bring passengers out of the station. Also, while buses were dispatched, it would not be feasible for buses to carry even a small percentage of the people leaving the affected stations.

Metro made every effort to keep its passengers informed of the incident and its impact on service. However, we recognize that information alone cannot compensate for the difficulties the situation presented to a large number of commuters. We genuinely regret any problems this may have caused you, and thank you for your understanding and continued patronage.

Sincerely,

David L. Gunn

David L. Gunn
General Manager

A PUBLIC TRANSPORTATION PARTNERSHIP OF THE DISTRICT OF COLUMBIA, MARYLAND AND VIRGINIA

Letters of Recommendation

Letters of recommendation usually follow a useful, well-established form. In writing one, you should do the following:

- State the name of the person and the role or position you are recommending the person for.
- Explain how long, and in what capacity, you have known the person.
- Identify the individual's skills, knowledge, experience, or work habits. (Consider what information the recipient of the letter will find helpful.)
- Mention a couple of qualities that make the individual special.
- Reiterate your recommendation.

Depending on how well you know the person you are recommending, how enthusiastic you are about recommending him or her, and whom the letter is going to, you may want to reorganize the parts or develop some portions in greater (or lesser) detail.

Be as specific as possible. If you state that someone "takes initiative and follows through," provide substantiation: "When Claudia realized that the department would be converting to flextime, she polled employees as to their preferences, worked out a schedule, presented it for approval, and then introduced the program to employees."

Striking the right tone is difficult. You need to sound enthusiastic without being gushy. Too many superlatives lend a note of insincerity. Above all, maintain a balance between your desire to help a deserving individual and your obligation to maintain the integrity of your profession or organization, and your own good name.

See the next page for an example of a letter of recommendation.

RALLY CORPORATION

March 1, 1996

Ms. Mary Louise Clare
Executive Vice President
Expert Systems, Inc.
6678 Avenue B
Albany, NY 12005-5790

Dear Ms. Clare:

I'm pleased to recommend Bill Coates as a design consultant for your firm.
Bill totally renovated three of our plants in the past five years. He is now
hard at work on a fourth plant.

We hired Bill because of his reputation for retaining the architectural
integrity of old well-designed buildings. He deserves the reputation he has
earned. Our plants have been featured in several architectural magazines.
The buildings are not only beautiful; they are also functional.

Bill remains involved in a project from start to finish. He oversees the
construction and keeps management informed of its progress. He's proud of
his work and likes to drive by "just to see how things are coming along." In
my opinion, he's the best in the field.

Give me a call if would like further information, and do feel free to come by
and see his work for yourself.

Sincerely,

Thomas Vitka

Thomas Vitka
Vice President, Buildings and Grounds

9 KENILWORTH ROAD
ALBANY, NY 12007-5732
(518) 795-9500

Delivering Unwelcome News

It's not easy to be the bearer of unwelcome news, but some writers make the task harder than necessary. They either adopt a false, overapologetic tone that makes the reader feel patronized, or they so mask the message that the reader feels duped. One should not go to the opposite extreme, however, and become blunt, unfeeling, or brutal.

Bad news is a fact of everyday business life. Businessmen and women are usually mature enough to want it straight. They also want reasons for the news. They even want a little humanity in the way they are given the news.

Sometimes you may find it easier to communicate the news in person or on the phone, for you can easily soften the message with your tone of voice. A spoken message may also come across with less authority and finality than a written message.

When you do write, avoid sandwiching the bad news between an irrelevant, indirect, or overly cushioned beginning and ending. Avoid overstating your sorrow. Avoid making upbeat statements that attempt to force goodwill on the reader who is really not in the mood to be a jolly-good sport.

In most cases you can do the following:

- State the context.
- Tell the reader the unwelcome news.
- Give specific reasons for your denial.
- Offer alternatives or encouragement, if appropriate.
- End courteously.

See page 85 for an example of this type of letter.

NEW YORK UNIVERSITY

SCHOOL OF LAW

Committee on Admissions
40 Washington Square South, New York, New York 10012

March 25, 1995

Mr. John Doe
125 Auburn Street
Cambridge, MA 02138

Dear Mr. Doe:

　　The Committee on Admissions has carefully considered your application. I am sorry to inform you that we are unable to offer you admission to the School of Law. Since more than 6,600 candidates competed for admission this year, the Committee has had to make many difficult choices.

　　We hope you understand that our decision on your application is not an estimate of your potential as a law student or an attorney. Since the vast majority of our applicants are clearly capable of success in law school and beyond, we inevitably must turn away many who will succeed in law simply for lack of space in our class.

　　Please accept our best wishes for your educational and career success.

Sincerely,

Nan McNamara
Assistant Dean for Admissions

A private university in the public service

Letters of Complaint

When you're dissatisfied with products, services, and policies, *do* take the time to put your complaint in writing. Not only does a letter force the recipient to deal with the issue, but it also forces you to deal with the issue logically and completely.

Complaint letters are easy to write, though controlling your emotions is not so easy. Since an angry or scolding tone may work against you, attempt to empty yourself of your ugliest feelings before sitting down to write.

The letter should be simple and firm. After identifying the purpose for your writing, you need to cover three basic points:

- The problem—what happened or didn't happen.
- The cost—in terms of inconvenience, aggravation, or money.
- The solution—the remedy you suggest.

You must, of course, supply adequate details so that the reader can fully understand the situation. Dates, places, times, names of people involved, and pertinent numbers (purchase order, invoice, or model) are among the facts you should include.

In an initial complaint, at least, it pays to assume goodwill on the part of the organization you are dealing with and to expect that it will wish to rectify the situation. Most companies willingly correct what went wrong or, if that is impossible, explain why the situation occurred.

The letter on the next page uses the approach recommended. While the letter shows displeasure, it focuses on the facts:

Southern Industrial   9 Lee Drive   Three Oaks, GA 30352   (404) 250-6900

February 16, 1996

Alphonse Geller
Ace Service
300 Wilson Boulevard
Atlanta, GA 30346

Dear Mr. Geller:

We were recently overcharged by your company for repairs made to three of our copy machines.

On January, 26, 1996, Mr. Eng, of your firm, visited our plant in Three Oaks to estimate the cost of overhauling our copy machines. According to him, three of our machines required servicing at a cost of $100 to $150 per machine, depending on how many parts needed replacement. (I have enclosed a copy of his estimate.)

On February 9, Mr. Sacks and Mr. Cruz repaired the machines and left a bill for $629 (copy enclosed). This bill exceeds your maximum estimate by $179.

I called Mr. Eng on February 12 to question the bill. He said the costs were higher than estimated because the work took longer than expected. But according to the estimate, the cost depended on the number of new parts, not on the time spent at our plant.

Please issue us a revised bill that is in line with your original estimate. Please also itemize the bill to show the repairs made to, and the parts replaced on, each of the machines.

Sincerely,

John Lamartine

John Lamartine
Plant Manager

Enclosures

Responses to Letters of Complaint

People who take the time to write letters of complaint are entitled to a courteous and prompt reply. No matter whether the complaint is justified or not, you should answer in a responsible, professional way. Never trivialize the situation or belittle your reader, even if he or she seems to be a grumbler.

In answering complaints, you should do four things: acknowledge, explain, reassure, and apologize.

Acknowledge. First, acknowledge that the person has a right to complain. If the complaint is justified, you can begin your letter by stating that the customer is right: "Your records are correct. We overstated your tax bill by $212.00." If, on the other hand, the complaint is unjustified, you can, at the very least, thank the customer for having brought the matter to your attention: "Thank you for taking the time to let us know about your experiences using our product."

Explain. Find out what happened and explain it. A person rarely tires of reading a response to his or her complaint. And by taking the time to explain thoroughly what happened, you come across as being concerned and conscientious. Avoid citing company policy to explain why something did or did not happen, unless you explain why that policy is necessary. If your explanation involves admitting that your company was wrong, consult your legal department. Issues involving liability can be tricky.

Reassure. Let your reader know that the situation has been, or is being, resolved. Avoid saying that the problem will not recur unless you are sure it will not. If you cannot resolve the problem to your reader's satisfaction, at least reassure him or her that you have done your best.

Apologize. Say you are sorry for the person's trouble, inconvenience, or frustration.

People are usually reasonable, especially if you have been sincere and honest. Well-worded responses can win back your reader's loyalty and restore the goodwill felt toward you and your company.

Benjamin Hayes, Packaging and Distribution Manager at the *St. Petersburg Times,* received the letter of complaint on the next page. His response follows on page 90.

79 Freedom Place
Palm Harbor, FL 34684
November 21,1995

St. Petersburg Times
490 First Avenue South
St. Petersburg, FL 33701

Dear Production Manager:

I can't understand why the sections in your Sunday paper are
placed in a different order every week. Every Sunday I have
to dig through the paper looking for the sections I like to
read. Usually the travel, comics, and ads are in the front.
Sections A, B, and C are way in the back—and they are not
even in alphabetical order. It's aggravating.

I recently moved here from Detroit. The Detroit News arrived
every week organized the way I like to read it. The News is a
large newspaper like yours, yet they take a lot more care in
putting together the sections.

Isn't there anything you can do?

                         Sincerely,

                         Madeline Hardy

                         Madeline Hardy

St. Petersburg Times

Benjamin Hayes
Packaging and Distribution Manager

November 27, 1995

Ms. Madeline Hardy
79 Freedom Place
Palm Harbor, FL 34684

Dear Ms. Hardy:

Thank you for letting us know about the problems caused by your Sunday paper not being in a logical sequence. I agree that having to sort through the whole paper to find the sections of most interest can be aggravating. Unfortunately, deadlines for sections, machine capacity, and even the number of slick inserts dictate how we package the paper. I would like to say that there is an easy solution, but there is not.

Some years ago our paper was assembled by more than 900 carriers in 45 districts; it is now assembled by machines in a central control area. By centralizing processing, we feel we can guarantee our readers and advertisers product accuracy, but the trade-off is a less organized paper.

We start "building" packages six days in advance of publication using the sections that are printed earliest to hold the preprinted advertisements. As you noted, the Comics and Travel sections usually hold these ads. Later in the week, other sections are added to the pack. Finally, before delivering your paper, your carrier adds Sections A, B, C and your local section to the machine-made packet.

You mentioned you did not have this problem with the *Detroit News*. I was curious how they were able to sort their paper so carefully. I talked with Dick Fischer, my counterpart at the Detroit Newspapers. Dick told me that they send more parts to the carriers to insert by hand. He mentioned, however, that they will be installing additional inserting equipment soon; thus, they will be packaging the paper as we do.

The building of the Sunday paper is easier to show than to explain in a letter. If at any time you would like a tour of our production facility, I would be happy to show you around. I will pass your letter to the Packaging Manager to see if she can find a way to sort the paper more consistently week to week.

Sincerely,

B. Hayes

c: Ralph Imhof, Production Director
Diane Constantino, Packaging Manager

Letters of Request

Much of our business writing consists of asking people to do something. Sometimes the recipients of these letters are eager to comply with the request. For example, if you write to a resort inquiring about using their site for your next convention, they will respond quickly, in hopes of obtaining your business. Yet, at other times, readers may not be so eager to comply because complying may cause them some inconvenience or expense. For example, you may be asking co-workers to assist you in developing an internship program, or you might be asking your boss to purchase new software that has not been budgeted. Several simple rules of thumb can help you get positive responses.

Give complete information. Anticipate questions the reader might ask. Remember, the reader may not know things that you take for granted. If you provide the right information and details, including the date by which the information is needed, your reader will be able to respond quickly—without endless games of telephone tag.

Tell your reader why you are asking him or her to do something. A simple "because" lets your reader know that you have a good reason for making your request. Giving a reason is particularly important when you are inconveniencing the reader.

Point out any benefits to the reader. If responding to your request will in any way benefit your reader, make that benefit explicit.

Make your letter easy to skim and easy to respond to. If you are asking questions in your letter, use a list format so that your reader can go right down the list in responding to your questions. If you are asking readers for a short response—to sign up for an event, for example—include a tear-off response form at the bottom.

Use a courteous tone. Sometimes in asking people to do something, you are really *telling* them to do something. For example, you might be "asking" departments to get closing figures to you earlier than usual. Using "please" and "thank you" is always appropriate. Using a bossy tone might put readers off—and some might stubbornly refuse to answer, simply because of a demanding tone.

The memo on page 92 asks employees to give blood. The writer tells them why giving blood is important. He follows up the written request with a personal visit.

SHOWTIME NETWORKS INC.

Corporate Affairs

To: New York Corporate Affairs Staff
From: Chris Montpetit *Chris*
Date: October 19, 1994
Subject: *BLOOD DRIVE -- NOVEMBER 3*

SHOWTIME is sponsoring a blood drive on November 3rd. If you can give 45-60 minutes of your time to donate blood, you will be helping as many as <u>five</u> people who are fighting for their health or their lives.

As one of this year's Blood Drive Captains, I encourage you to give blood. Our blood drive will be held <u>Thursday, November 3rd, from 10:00 A.M. - 3:30 P.M., on the Concourse Level here at 1633 Broadway</u>. Donating blood is more important than ever . . . and it's actually very easy.

Anyone who registers will be eligible to win one of three raffle prizes--a pair of Broadway tickets (to the show of your choice), a Casio portable television, or a Vivitar camera.

Did you know that 95% of us will have used blood or a blood product by the time we're 72. Every day more than 2,000 pints of blood are needed in over 250 hospitals in the greater New York/New Jersey area. Because of a shortage in our area, 30% of the needed blood comes from other regions in the U.S. and Europe.

I'm hoping you will consider giving blood during this year's drive. Your donation could help to save up to <u>five</u> lives! I will be stopping by in the next day or so to distribute information booklets and to answer any questions you may have. Thanks.

Persuasion: Some Practical Pointers

Persuading another person to your point of view is a difficult—but not impossible—task. You will, of course, have to present solid facts and logical arguments to win over your reader, but before deciding on what facts you'll present, step back and assess your chance of success. Then, once you have a realistic idea of your potential to succeed, plan a strategy that incorporates some common sense. Do not get so carried away with developing evidence for your case that you forget the more human aspects of persuasion.

ASSESS YOUR CHANCES OF SUCCESS

Your chance of succeeding will improve if you take the time to analyze three variables—your reader's readiness to accept your position, his or her bias toward your position, and your credibility with your reader.

Your reader's readiness. Readers act only when they are ready to; thus, part of your task will be to bring your reader to the point where he or she can comfortably say "yes." In some cases your reader may not have sufficient knowledge about an issue. Before you launch into strong arguments in favor of your position, you will have to step back, relay some of the basics, and stress the importance of the issue. Then, in a second memo, you can present evidence in support of your position. In another case, your reader may consider the issue important, but, because of other limitations or priorities, may not be ready to hear your case. You'll have to delay your appeal or show your reader why the issue demands immediate attention.

Your reader's bias. Ask yourself where your reader stands on the issue. If he or she is *favorably inclined,* you can state your position or recommendation at once, develop a few strong reasons, and focus on motivating action.

If your reader is *neutral or indifferent,* begin with your recommendation, develop several arguments, especially those that the reader will find compelling, and then, perhaps, motivate action. Be sure you are practical, moderate, and objective. Most sophisticated audiences want to hear a balanced argument, that is, the pros and cons. By being objective, you also enhance your credibility.

If your reader is *negatively inclined,* you may not want to lead off with your recommendation. First set the context and advance your strongest arguments (those that will appeal most to your reader), making sure that your evidence is sound and your reasoning airtight. If your reader is able to poke holes in your argument, you will lose your case. Make your recommendation only after you have worn down some of your reader's resistance. Try to discover the reasons for the person's bias. This knowledge may give you some clues for additional arguments or for alternative approaches.

Your credibility. If your reader thinks you are highly credible, you will stand a good chance of convincing him or her—all other factors being equal. If your credibility is unestablished or low, rely heavily on strong factual evidence. Consider having someone else sign the document—someone with high credibility, of course, or get others whom your reader respects to buy into your idea first. You will, in this case, borrow credibility to help you make a convincing case.

USE SOME COMMON SENSE

Facts alone rarely convince. Facts, together with an approach sensitive to your reader's personal and business needs, will more likely convince. Develop the facts, rather than simply listing them, and always point out specific benefits to the reader. Avoid making sweeping statements. For example, instead of saying that your plan is better than the existing plan, tell *why* it is better. And avoid cliches like "I'm sure you will agree." Instead, present your reader with well-thought-out arguments so that he or she will say "I agree that this is a good idea" after reading your memo. Throughout, practice three virtues: patience, prudence, and flexibility.

Patience. Seldom will you persuade your reader in a single attempt. The process can take time and multiple attempts. Some may be written, some oral, some formal, some informal. Courting your reader demands patience.

Prudence. Be careful not to push your ideas too hard—especially if your reader is not immediately taken with them. If your pursuit is unrelenting, your reader might become stubborn. Be careful, too, not to make promises you can't keep, and don't exaggerate. If you inflate just one fact or figure, and your reader realizes it, he or she will question other assertions as well.

Flexibility. When you realize you may not get all of what you want, you may have to make a few concessions. Decide if getting some of what you want is better than getting none. If you can concede a point or two, do so, but not too soon. You do not want to weaken your own case. Keep an open, friendly dialogue with the person you are trying to convince. By determining the sticking points, you may be able to modify your approach or negotiate some of the details.

(Also see "Shaping a Persuasive Message" below.)

Shaping a Persuasive Message

Various theories of persuasion have been advanced through the centuries. Analyzing how people think and why they act has prompted serious inquiry. In our own times, advertisers—experts in persuasion—have adapted several theoretical models. Further adapting their approach can help us shape our persuasive messages.

Advertisers first get their audience's attention; then they introduce the idea or product they are selling. They develop convincing evidence; finally, they motivate action.

Get the audience's attention.   Before a reader can be persuaded, his or her attention must be engaged. Advertisers appeal to basic human needs—physical, emotional, psychic. In getting a business person's attention, you'll want to consider the business's goals or needs.

If the business is "for-profit," you'll likely get your reader's attention if you appeal to making, or saving, money. You can also provoke interest by appealing to efficiency, productivity, competitive advantage. Consider also the values of the company, department, or person you are writing to. If safety, high morale, or teamwork are important, you may want to use one of these attention-getting devices in your opening. If the business is "not-for-profit," focus on the overall goals or mission of the organization, but make the attention-getter specific and action-oriented. In either case, be careful not to be cute. Sometimes, you can begin directly with a recommendation. It, in and of itself, will get the reader's attention.

Introduce the product or idea.   Let the reader know what you are recommending early on. You may want to make a specific recommendation ("I recommend that we rent 20,000 square feet of warehouse space in Laramie") or a broad recommendation ("We need to look at ways to streamline our procedures so that we will meet the deadline"). Your reader's attitude or bias will help you decide how general or specific you should be. (See "Persuasion: Some Practical Pointers" on pages 93–94.)

Develop convincing evidence. In this section, you'll answer the question "why should we do this?" Choose a few of the best reasons, those you consider important and those your reader will consider important. Mentioning a fact is not enough. You need to make it real to your reader. Advertisers and salespeople speak in terms of "features" and "benefits." In selling a product, a salesperson will point out a feature, make it real to the client, and spell out its benefits. "The calculator measures 2 x 3 inches, small enough to fit in the palm of your hand, small enough to put in your pocket and take to work. . . ." Develop your ideas similarly. Name a feature, make it real, point out its specific benefits.

Though an advertisement never points out weaknesses of a product or ways it is not as good as the competition's, do not be afraid to mention some of your concerns. No product or idea is perfect. If you over-represent or misrepresent your product or idea, your reader may question your objectivity, and thus your credibility.

Motivate action. Once you've sold your idea, you'll want to make it easy for your reader to act, and to act quickly. Advertisers make it easy for you to buy their product ("Call this toll-free number and we'll send you . . ." or "This product is available at. . . "). They also try to get you to act quickly, before the effect of their message has worn off ("Sale ends Friday . . ." or "While supply lasts. . . ").

In motivating action in a persuasive memo, consider what steps will need to be taken if your reader says "yes." Structure the action in terms of what you, or others will do. Try to leave little, if any, implementation to your reader. If you've proposed renting more warehouse space, you might end your memo by saying, "I'll call Jack Roman, the broker who found us lab space last spring. I'll look at some of the sites and report back to you." If you think motivating action at this stage will be perceived as being aggressive, hold off. First get a response from the reader and motivate later—in writing or orally—when the person is ready to move ahead.

In the memo on pages 97–98, Hugh McDonough, a trusted employee, recommends hiring another secretary. He ties his recommendation to two important departmental projects. He justifies his recommendation and shows how and when it would be implemented. His boss, Valerie Wilde, is open-minded and efficient. She likes brief, comprehensive memos.

To:	Valerie Wilde		January 15, 1996

To: Valerie Wilde   *H/n D*   January 15, 1996

From: Hugh McDonough   Copies to: R. Brown
                                                     C. Manzetti

Subject: Hiring Another Secretary   A. Tinsley

This spring we will begin working on two important projects: hosting the sales conference in September and meeting the November deadline for the new catalogue. These projects will give us visibility within the industry and community, and among our present and potential clients.

I recommend we hire a secretary by the end of March. We can train this person before summer, when we will need coverage for vacations and when our preparation for the conference will be intense. By summer's end, we will need to plan the catalogue and assign writing tasks. An experienced secretary will cost from $26,000 to $32,500 (including overhead).

This addition to our staff will ensure that we have a trained, dedicated secretary who can support our efforts in these activities.

Benefits to the Department

Keeping up with the workload. Last year our workload increased by about 15%, though we did not increase our staff. For the past three years, our workload has increased at nearly the same rate as our sales increase. Projections for 1996 show sales increasing 8% to 10%; thus, our workload will increase by about the same amount. Hiring another secretary will alleviate our backlog and allow us to keep up with the increased workload.

Adding new skills to the department. We should hire someone with skills our existing staff does not now provide. We especially need someone who knows PageMaker (we can use PageMaker for much of the catalogue) and who can prepare professional-looking charts and graphs that we need for so many of our meetings.

Increasing productivity. You and Bob have approved overtime and hiring temps, but these measures will no longer be sufficient. Staff are not as productive after hours as they are from 9:00 to 5:00. Though temps are cheaper (we pay $19.50 an hour) than a full-time employee, they are less productive; moreover, because they need guidance from regular staff, they interrupt the work of others. Once trained, a new secretary will help us increase our productivity, and our costs for overtime and temps will be substantially eliminated.

Cost Analysis

Costs for overtime and temps. Costs for overtime and temps for the last two years and my projections for this year are as follows:

	1994	1995	Year-to-year Increase	Projected 1996 (+46%)
Overtime	$5,800	$8,400	+45%	$12,180
Temps	6,400	9,500	+48%	14,060
	$12,200	$17,800	+46%	$26,240

The above projection assumes the same rate increase for 1996—a conservative estimate, given the projects and our increased workload.

Cost of a new secretary. The salary for an experienced secretary ranges from $20,000 to $25,000. Benefits (30% added to salary) would raise our costs to $26,000 to $32,500.

Instead of spending money this year on overtime and temps, we can hire a new secretary. If we are able to hire someone for $26,000 (salary plus benefits) our costs would be less than the projected pay-out for overtime and temps. If we pay top dollar, $32,500, our costs will be minimal—no more than $6,260.

Implementation

Reassignments. Beginning in March, a staff member will need to devote full time to coordinating the new projects. Anne is willing, and is certainly able, to assume these projects. The new secretary could cover for vacationing staff (a good way to learn about the department) and begin working on the catalogue, under Anne's supervision. Joe will be graduating in May and will work full time until Labor Day. When he leaves, the new person would assume his tasks.

Space. Temps now use the desk and computer under the bulletin board, but this space is inadequate for full-time use. The office is already cramped. Perhaps Vinnie can suggest a better arrangment. I'll call him.

Next Steps

If you give me the go ahead, I will write a job description and work out a hiring schedule with Human Resources. I will ask Anne to review resumes and do some initial interviewing. Can we talk later this week?

The Sales Letter

Sales letters take various forms, depending on the product or service you are selling and on the audience you are addressing. The sales effort usually takes place in stages. Some of your exchanges with the potential client will be oral; some will be written. Your goal in selling is to match what you have (your product or service) with what the potential client needs. And sometimes you'll even create a need, for your audience may not have considered ways your product can enhance their personal or professional lives. Knowing your audience and their needs will enable you to point out the uses and benefits of your product.

Two kinds of letters—the initial sales letter and the follow-up letter—are common to most selling efforts. Here are a few suggestions for writing these letters.

THE INITIAL SALES LETTER

Initially you will probably send a short letter telling your reader about your product or service. This letter is generally accompanied by enclosures—brochures, testimonials, write-ups—that give additional information about your company or product.

In this letter, describe what you are selling and focus on the benefits it will provide to your reader. Your purpose in this initial letter is not necessarily to sell; rather, it is to provoke some interest on the part of your reader. Most actual selling is done in person, on the phone, or by means of another letter or two. The process is rarely swift.

This initial letter may follow the general approach presented in the previous chapter (see "Shaping a Persuasive Message" on pages 95–96), though in abbreviated form. Focus on quickly getting your reader's attention and on clearly stating what you are offering. Point out a few benefits, but make sure they are not broad, bland, or overblown.

Brevity can work to your benefit. Short letters (one page in this case) are usually skimmed or read. Longer ones end up at the bottom of the pile. And if you keep the letter short, your reader will not get caught up in too much detail. He or she will know what you do and how it might help. The letter must be well crafted—so that it will stand out in the reader's mind.

When your reader receives your letter, he or she may call you to find out more about the product, or you may call the reader. Once the reader's interest is piqued, you will want to learn as much as you can about his or her needs. Listening well, asking questions, and finding out the potential client's present needs will help you begin matching what you have, or can offer, with what the client wants.

Following this exchange, you will often write one or more follow-up letters that develop features especially relevant to your reader.

THE FOLLOW-UP LETTER(S)

Once the potential client is interested, you can begin showing your product at its best, always matching its features and benefits to the client's needs. This carefully reasoned letter should be objective and specific. After reading this letter, your reader should be able to say, "Now I understand the product or service the company offers, how I can use it, and how it will benefit me." With a few more follow-up letters or phone calls, you'll eventually want your reader to say, "I now also understand why this product is better for us than other products. I know what it will not provide. I also know about its cost, guarantees. . . . "

In ending a follow-up letter, try to stay in control of the issue by saying that you will call or by looking toward the next step. Avoid ending the letter with cliches ("Please do not hesitate to call me if you have any questions") that leave the next step to the reader. Keep in charge of the issue, gently, without becoming a nag.

The selling effort, much like any wooing process, usually takes time; moreover, the client's interest may diminish, then grow. But the wooing should not become tedious or drawn out. The eventual "yes" will come if you have targeted the right audience and shown how your product will benefit them.

The letter on the next page follows up on a previous conversation with a potential client. It describes what the company does and suggests ways the client might use its services. (This letter was sent by facsimile; the information mentioned in the letter was sent by regular mail.)

Paul R. Heinerscheid
President and CEO

SATELLITE NETWORK SYSTEMS

2375 University Avenue West
St. Paul, Minnesota 55114-1603
(612) 644-2200   Fax (612) 644-8025

August 22, 1994

via telefax #371-9189
and regular mail (with enclosures)

Ms. Gloria McLenihan
Minnesota Meetings
c/o Marecek Cairns & Yelsey
730 Second Avenue, Suite 281
Minneapolis, MN 55402

Dear Gloria:

I enjoyed meeting you at the French American Chamber of Commerce last Thursday and wanted to follow up on our short, but very pleasant, conversation about what we call "business television."

Specifically, I wanted to let you know of the capabilities of my company, Satellite Network Systems (SNS), in areas that might interest Minnesota Meetings or Marecek Cairns & Yelsey.

SNS offers customer-friendly, end-to-end video communications services. Our clients are corporations and organizations who need real-time, live, interactive television services to one or multiple locations simultaneously.

Minnesota Meetings might use our services if one of its speakers is unable to make it to the Twin Cities or has to cancel at the last minute. You might want to invite an additional speaker and bring him or her to your meeting by means of our video conferencing services. You might also envision broadcasting meetings to several additional sites within the state, nationally, or even internationally. Your public relations firm might even launch a new product or service to a national audience from a single origination point.

Satellite Network Systems has handled many such events, always with great success. We would be glad to discuss the possibilities of your using video communications. I am sending, by regular mail, information that illustrates our use of this technology.

We will be broadcasting an event for MLMIC next Tuesday, August 30, at 10:00 a.m. Please join us at our offices if you'd like to see how business television works.

Best regards,

Paul R. Heinerscheid

101

International Correspondence

As American companies expand beyond their borders, their employees need to become aware of the way business is conducted in other countries. The American way may not necessarily prevail, even if the language used is English. Ways of communicating often differ markedly from one country to the next; thus, if you are writing (or speaking) to colleagues in another country, become aware of their norms. Your effectiveness may depend on your sensitivity to cultural differences.

Reviewing correspondence sent by your international colleagues can give you some clues about their approach to writing. While you will not want to mimic their writing, you will want to be aware of the differences. Modify your approach if it is far different from the intended readers'. First consider your relationship. Then look at the openings, the organization, style, and tone of their letters.

Your relationship. In many cultures, a business relationship is far different from a personal relationship. Though you may have met a business colleague several times, you should not assume that you are friends. Even if you use a person's first name when speaking, you may want to use his or her last name when writing. Ordinarily you will want to use the person's title, as well. Look at your correspondent's writing, if you can, and take that person's lead. Business relationships in other countries are often more formal than they are in the States.

Openings. Most readers in the United States will expect you to get down to business at once. But this directness can offend readers from other countries, where getting down to business immediately is not the norm. Customs differ. People of some nationalities start with personal greetings; others write, almost poetically, about the season. While it would be inappropriate to begin as they do, you may want to ease into your subject rather than boldly announcing it. (Telexes, e-mail, and faxes are notable exceptions. These forms of communication dictate a direct approach.)

Organization. If you are responding to a letter, let your correspondent's ordering of ideas guide you. If you are initiating correspondence, you are usually better off using a traditional mode of organization. Start with the context and background. Develop points sequentially. Take your reader through your reasoning before you advance recommendations.

Style. The words you choose largely determine your style. When writing to international audiences you may need to use formal or standard words instead of less formal language, slang, and idioms. Within the States, expressions like "getting up to speed" or "a hands-on approach" are acceptable in all but very formal documents, but a foreigner may not understand them or may feel they are too casual for a business letter. Idiomatic sentences like "give me a ballpark estimate" or "we're back to square one" may need to be restated or explained. Use jargon or specialized vocabulary if your reader understands it. Your style does not have to be simplistic (many non-native speakers of English know the language well), but it should be appropriate in terms of its level of formality. (See "Editing for Language, Style, and Tone" on pages 40–59.)

Tone. Your tone depends not only on the words you use, but also on the information you convey. Setting deadlines, no matter how polite your wording, may be considered brusque, and an overly zealous persuasive appeal may sound aggressive to someone who is used to a softer sell. Strong words like "must" and "should" carry a demanding tone. Adopting a humorous tone may trivialize the situation; more often than not, humor is misunderstood or inappropriate. Before sending your letter, look at the tone of the words you have chosen. Are they unnecessarily strong? Are they curt? Are they condescending or falsely polite? Or are they pointlessly humorous? The message conveyed by tone is often more potent than the message conveyed by information.

When writing to an international audience, be yourself, but also extend yourself. Find out about cultural and business norms in countries with which you do business. Doing business successfully—either in the United States or abroad—requires sensitivity to the ways others do business.

Note: If you correspond with colleagues from many countries, you may want to subscribe to a monthly newsletter, *Worldwide Business Practices Report*. Its purpose is to help executives familiarize themselves with international business practices and protocol. The newsletter is published by International Cultural Enterprises (1–800–626–2772).

Messages for Electronic Mail (E-mail)

Electronic mail (e-mail) systems turn computers into in-boxes. E-mail is used widely for internal and external messages and suits itself particularly well to short informal messages. Increasingly, organizations are adopting e-mail as the primary mode of internal communication. Some organizations have policies in place that treat e-mail as a business asset, not a personal asset; thus from a legal perspective, e-mail is admissable in court. It should, therefore, be given the same attention as traditional forms of correspondence.

In writing these messages, you can depart from some common writing conventions, but make sure that the speed the technology provides does not cause you to become careless. Veteran users of e-mail offer the following suggestions and cautions.

Address one topic per e-mail message. Many people reply to e-mail as they read it; thus, it is easier for them to respond if you discuss only one topic per message. If you introduce several topics, they may postpone responding until they can address all the topics covered.

Write an informative subject line. Phrase the subject line so that it tells the reader *what to do* in addition to *what the message is about*. A subject line may read "Send year-end figures to Joe ASAP" or "Proceed with distribution of vaccine." A precise subject line can prompt a reader to read your message before others.

Keep screen length in mind when organizing. Organize your message so that the most important information fits on the first screen. Remember, if your message goes onto a second or third screen, earlier screens are no longer visible to your reader. Avoid long messages.

Make it easy for your reader to respond. Word a message so that the reader can get back to you with a "yes/no" answer or a short response. Where possible, use questions instead of statements. Instead of saying, "Let me know your thoughts on Cory's proposal," ask "Should we adopt Cory's proposal?"

When you respond to an e-mail message, include the context in your reply. Even if you read a message and respond to it quickly, your colleague may not read your response immediately. The topic may no longer be fresh in his or her mind. The "reply" feature on most e-mail systems allows you to reply to a message *and* attach the original document. To save your reader time, you can, instead, include enough of the context so that your response will be instantly clear. Rather than simply replying, "Yes, let's go with your plan," say "Yes, let's go with your plan to use four-color ads in the West Coast edition."

Be concise. Use phrases or sentences, short words, and abbreviations, but be careful that your message is not so cryptic that it must be decoded or so terse that it seems rude. Make sure too that your style is not so disjointed that you would be embarrassed if your message were read by a wide audience.

Re-read your message in various tones of voice to prevent misunderstandings. Whenever you write, you control meaning—and tone—solely by the words you choose. Your tone of voice, your facial expressions, your gestures are all absent. The recipient of your message can read meaning into your message, a meaning you may not intend. Try reading the following sentence in various tones of voice—a neutral tone, a sarcastic tone, and a complimentary tone: "Your proposal was everything we expected." Since the meaning might be ambiguous without the tonal quality of the spoken language, re-word the message so that it cannot be misunderstood. If you intend to compliment your reader, for example, why not say, "Your proposal was excellent; it was everything we expected." (This is a good technique to use for any sort of writing, but it is especially important in e-mail, which is quick and conversational.)

Don't forget that many people may read your message. Just like regular correspondence, e-mail can be forwarded by the receiver (by the push of a button) or printed and distributed; moreover, with the growing popularity of on-line services, e-mail is becoming a collaborative means of communication. Make sure that the message shows you at your best.

Don't be too quick to push the "Send" button. Think seriously about what you've written and the reaction it is likely to produce *before* you send a message—especially if you are in a highly charged emotional state. Unlike regular correspondence, e-mail cannot be retrieved from the out-box or mail room.

Don't send highly confidential messages. Even if you delete a message, it is not erased from the system's memory. With networks like the Internet, your message may be stored on many different computers before it reaches its destination. There is no guarantee of security anywhere along the network.

Realize that e-mail cannot fully replace the need for other forms of communication. Because readers usually skim several e-mail messages, yours may not get the attention it deserves. At times, readers may not even remember reading a message, for the process is so quick. Sending a memo might be preferable. Handling the piece of paper may slow your reader down a bit and give added emphasis, and importance, to your message. In other cases, you may need to follow up an e-mail message with a phone call. Some readers may not reply to your message even if you have asked them to.

Thanks to Stever Robbins of Harvard Business School for major contributions to this chapter and to Kurt Rao of Viacom, Inc. for his suggestions.

A Glossary of Grammar and Usage

Your grammar and usage should be correct for two reasons—clarity and credibility. An ungrammatical sentence or a misused word can confuse or distract your readers and can cause you to look bad. Like bad manners, bad grammar and usage reflect your background and, perhaps, your educational level. Mistakes can lessen the opinion your readers hold of you and can lead them to question your expertise in other matters.

This glossary explains points of grammar and usage that perplex many business writers.

a, an

The use of *a* or *an* is dictated not by the first letter of the word that follows but by its initial sound. *A* precedes words beginning with consonant sounds (a meeting, a proposal). *An* precedes words beginning with vowel sounds (an announcement, an itinerary). Thus *a historian, a utility,* and *a one-year lease* are correct because the words following the article begin with consonant sounds—*h, y,* and *w. An honorable occasion, an NBC reporter,* and *an $80,000 salary* are correct because the sounds immediately following the articles are vowel sounds—*on, en,* and *ay.*

abbreviations

- Abbreviate titles when they precede or follow names but not when they appear without a name:

  Lt. Col. Daniels   Harold Remmer, M.D.   Carolyn Conroy, Ph.D.

  The lieutenant colonel was honored at a testimonial dinner.
  The doctor prescribed two aspirin and a good night's sleep.

- Abbreviate names of organizations, governmental agencies, companies, and some common terms. Periods are not generally used:

  PTA AFL-CIO FBI IBM AT&T GNP AWOL ID

  (Abbreviations that are pronounced as words—NOW, HUD, WASP—are called acronyms.)

- If your reader might be unfamiliar with an abbreviation or acronym, identify it the first time you use it. Put either the abbreviation or the unabbreviated form in parentheses:

  The company grants a Cost of Living Adjustment (COLA) each year.
  An ATM (Automated Teller Machine) will be installed in the lobby.

- Use the abbreviations *Co., Bros., Corp.,* and *Inc.* and the ampersand (&) with the name of the firm if the abbreviation is part of the official name of the company. Write the word out if you are using it without the name:

  White & Case   Aberdeen Co., Inc.
  but Boston Edison Company   The Forum Corporation
  The company is expanding into new markets.

- Avoid abbreviating months of the year, days of the week, cities, and the words *street, road,* or *avenue.* Abbreviate the names of states (use the two-letter abbreviations designated by the U.S. Postal Service) in addresses, but not within sentences.

  He will be moving to Warren, Michigan, in August. His address there will be
      3462 Bedford Road
      Warren, MI 48089.

- Avoid using Latin abbreviations, such as *i.e., e.g., viz.* Substitute English phrases (that is, for example, namely).

affect, effect

Affect, a verb, refers to an action. It is interchangeable with *change* or *influence:*

  The resignation of a veteran employee *affects* [changes] the unit's operation
      in several ways.
  The strike will *affect* [influence] shipments.
  The president's announcement *affected* [influenced] us profoundly.

Effect, a noun, is interchangeable with *a result* or *the result:*

> The resignation of a veteran employee has a number of *effects* [results] upon
> the unit's operation.
> What will the *effects* [results] of the strike be?
> The *effect* [result] of the president's announcement was startling.

The verb *to effect,* meaning *to bring about* or *to put into effect,* can be
replaced by the verb *to make.* In fact, using *make* is preferable; *to effect*
is a bit stilted.

> We will *effect* [bring about] this change as of the first of the year.
> We will *make* this change as of the first of the year.

bad/badly

Both "I feel bad" and "I feel badly" are correct, depending on what you
mean. "I feel bad" means "I'm sorry," or "I'm not well." "I feel
badly" means "My sense of touch is impaired."

> I feel bad because my raise didn't come through.
> My boss feels bad for me, too.

Both sentences are correct.

Confusion sets in because *badly* is used correctly in such sentences as
"Alfred has never spoken badly of you" and "The last shipment
arrived badly damaged." But *bad* follows certain verbs of sense—that is,
feel, look, taste, smell. Thus the following sentences are also correct:

> The last catalogue looked bad. The printing was smudged.
> This cream cheese tastes bad, but the bagel tastes good.
> The office smelled bad because he had just smoked a cheap cigar.

but—as first word in a sentence

There is no basis for objecting to the use of *but*—or any other word—at
the beginning of a sentence. But sentences beginning with *but* should
not be overused. They can change the pace of a series of sentences. And
they can add emphasis by forcing a reader to pause between two statements rather than run them together. Of 129 complete sentences on the
front page of the December 1, 1995, edition of *The New York Times,*
ten began with *but;* four began with *and.* (Headlines, captions, and
"Inside," which highlights stories in the paper, were excluded in the
count.) On the same day, of 72 complete sentences on the front page of
The Wall Street Journal, seven began with *but;* three began with *and.*

(Headlines, captions, and the "What's New" column, which summarizes important news items, were excluded in this count.)

comma splice

A comma splice occurs when a writer joins two sentences with a comma. What looks simply like an error in punctuation really constitutes an error in grammar. These sentences are *incorrect:*

> The audit was completed in June, thus the report should be out soon.
> These results are poor, however profits should rebound next year.

The comma splice is easy to correct. In the examples above, the sentences were joined by *thus* or *however.* These words and others like them *(nevertheless, consequently, furthermore, therefore, moreover...)* are called conjunctive adverbs. When a conjunctive adverb is used as a transition between two ideas, a period or semicolon (semicolons are more common) separates the two thoughts, and a comma follows the conjunctive adverb.

> The audit was completed in June. Thus, the report should be out soon.
> These results are poor; however, profits should rebound next year.

Coordinating conjunctions *(and, but, or, for, nor, yet),* with commas before them, may also be used to join sentences:

> These results are poor, but profits should rebound next year.
> Costs increased only slightly, and the profit margin remained stable.

Yet another, and often preferable, way to eliminate the comma splice is to recast the ideas by subordinating one idea to the other. By doing this, the relationship between ideas is more accurately expressed:

> Although these results are poor, profits should rebound next year.
> Because costs increased only slightly, the profit margin remained stable.

contractions

Style in business writing has relaxed considerably in the last decade. In many cases contractions are preferred since they make sentences sound natural. Listen to your writing. Hear how it sounds. Don't use so many contractions that they call attention to themselves, but don't avoid using them altogether, except, perhaps, in a very formal document.

dangling modifiers

If you begin a sentence with certain grammatical constructions (a participial phrase or an infinitive phrase), you'll have to look carefully at the sentence to make sure it is clear and correct.

Participial phrases begin with a participle (a word ending in *-ing, -en,* or *-ed):*

> Knowing little about finance,. . .
> Taken literally,. . .
> Viewed from management's perspective,. . .

An infinite phrase begins with the word *to*:

> To increase earnings,. . .

These phrases dangle when the noun or pronoun after the introductory phrase does not follow logically from the phrase:

> *Incorrect:*   Knowing little about finance, the numbers confused me.

The sentence above suggests that "the numbers" knew little about finance. To correct a dangling participle, make sure that <u>the first word</u> after the participial phrase relates to the information given in that introductory phrase:

> *Correct:*   Knowing little about finance, <u>I</u> was confused by the numbers.

If the sentence sounds awkward, revise it yet again:

> Because I knew little about finance, I was confused by the numbers.

> *Incorrect:*   Taken literally, we find the regulations to be quite strict.
> *Correct:*   Taken literally, <u>the regulations</u> seem quite strict.

> *Incorrect:*   Viewed from management's perspective, you might see the situation differently.
> *Correct:*   Viewed from management's perspective, <u>the situation</u> might seem quite different. *OR* If you view the situation from management's perspective, you might see it differently.

> *Incorrect:*   To increase earnings, sales must first improve.
> *Correct:*   To increase earnings, <u>we</u> must first improve sales.

data

Data is the Latin plural form of *datum.* In technical or scholarly writing, *data* is generally used as a plural: "The data were correct." In most business situations, however, *data* is used as a singular collective noun: "The data was correct."

fewer, less

The sign at the checkout counter in the supermarket reads "Less than ten items." It should read "Fewer than ten items."

Fewer refers to number and indicates "how many." It is used with plural nouns: *fewer dollars, fewer machines, fewer conflicts. Less* refers to amount and indicates "how much." It is used with singular nouns: *less money, less equipment, less conflict.*

if it was, if it were

The subjunctive form *were* is still used to express hypothetical, doubtful, or contrary-to-fact statements. *Were* is required in the following:

> If the company *were* to relocate. . .
> Assume your company *were* to go bankrupt. . .
> If a discounted rate *were* available. . .

More and more, *was* is used conversationally in such expressions as "If the company was to relocate, most employees would move." Such usage should be confined to informal speech. You may choose to say *was* in the sentence quoted above during a coffee break, but when you return to your desk to write, use *were.*

its, it's

It's (with an apostrophe) should be used only as a contraction for *it is.* Yet, surprisingly, many educated writers consistently misuse *it's* to indicate possession. *Its* is possessive, just like the words *his, hers,* and *ours* (all without apostrophes).

Note the correct use of the two words in the following passage:

> The company announced that *its* profits in the last quarter had exceeded expectations. As a result *its* dividend would be increased by four cents. "*It's* our intention to pass this earnings increase on to stockholders," the company president remarked.

me, myself, I

Most of the errors in the use of *me, myself,* and *I* result from an unconscious but widespread misconception that using *I* is unacceptable in business writing or from the equally false notion that *me* is somehow inelegant and should therefore be avoided. *Myself* becomes the all-purpose substitute.

Incorrect: Bob Ames and myself will continue to service your account.
Correct: Bob Ames and I will continue to service your account.

Incorrect: Call Bob or myself if you have any questions.
Correct: Call Bob or me if you have any questions.

If you are unsure of the correct usage of *me* or *I* in these cases, simply leave the other person out of the sentence and see which of the pronouns occurs naturally. Thus, you would say, "*I* will continue to service your account." When adding Bob to the sentence, keep the same pronoun, *I*. Similarly, "Call *me* if you have any questions." When adding Bob to the sentence, retain *me*.

Myself is used correctly as a reflexive pronoun or as an emphatic device. A reflexive pronoun shows that the doer and the receiver of an action are the same: "I hurt myself." When used for emphasis *myself* is interchangeable with "personally," as in "I myself would never have done that."

numbers

Write out numbers one through ten. Use figures for numbers over ten. Some exceptions apply:

- Use figures to refer to dates, addresses, time of day (except if the word *o'clock* is used), money, decimals, fractions, phone numbers, or page and footnote numbers.
- Use a figure-word combination when referring to large round numbers: 15 million inhabitants, a $12 billion deficit.
- When several numbers appear in the same paragraph, use the same form for consistency. (Figures, because they are quicker to read, are preferable.)
- When a figure begins a sentence, write the figure as a word or rephrase the sentence so that the figure does not appear at the beginning.
- When two numbers appear next to one another, use a figure for one and a word for the other (30 ten-pound packages, twelve 36-inch pipes).

Use the number twice, as in "Please sign the two (2) forms," only in legal contracts.

only

Only is often misplaced in sentences. One reason for its misplacement is the long oral tradition of placing *only* before the verb. Hence, sentences like the following sound natural:

He *only* sent the package yesterday.
We will *only* start the program if everyone approves it.

A reader generally interprets these sentences correctly, even though they could have meanings quite different from those intended. The first sentence could mean "Only he (no one else) sent the package" or "He didn't do anything yesterday but send the package." The second sentence could mean "If everyone approves the program, the only thing we'll do is start it."

By placing *only* as close as possible to what it modifies, you will not risk misinterpretation on the part of your reader.

When rewritten, the above sentences become precise, unambiguous, and correct:

He sent the package *only* yesterday.
We will start the program *only* if everyone approves it.

parallelism

Parallelism is the use of grammatically balanced forms to express two or more ideas of equal weight. Most writers can easily identify simple errors in parallelism. They would have little difficulty revising the following awkward sentence:

Incorrect: I like to identify a problem and solving it.
Correct: I like to identify a problem and solve it.

Lack of parallelism is harder to spot in more complicated constructions. It occurs most often in these grammatical situations:

• Where ideas are listed in a series:

Incorrect: The proposal was practical, reasonable in cost, and presented convincingly.
Correct: The proposal was practical, economical, and convincing.

Incorrect: The recommendations should be reviewed by branch managers and all who supervise.
Correct: The recommendations should be reviewed by branch managers and supervisors.

• Where ideas are connected by correlatives such as *either. . . or, neither. . . nor, not only. . . but also:*

Incorrect: Neither an increase in sales nor reducing the work force can solve the company's financial woes.

Correct: Neither increasing sales nor reducing the work force will solve the company's financial woes.

Incorrect: The provost was respected not only for her hard work and dedication, but also because she got along well with people.

Correct: The provost was respected not only for her hard work and dedication, but also for her ability to get along well with people.

prepositions, ending sentences with

Winston Churchill is widely credited with having had the last word on this matter. When he was criticized for having ended a sentence with a preposition, he penciled on a manuscript, "This is the type of arrant pedantry up with which I will not put."

H. W. Fowler, whose *Dictionary of Modern English Usage* (Oxford University Press, 1965) has long been recognized as the Bible in its field, labeled the idea that a preposition must not be used at the end of a sentence a "cherished superstition." These "notions of correctness," Fowler says, derived from Latin standards but have no validity in modern English. Ending a sentence with a preposition is entirely proper and, in fact, is preferred if it results in a clear, natural-sounding sentence:

It was the highest mortgage rate we had ever heard of.
Jones is someone worth talking to.

The alternatives are tongue twisters: "It was the highest mortgage rate of which we had ever heard." "Jones is someone with whom it is worthwhile to talk."

On the other hand, the end of a sentence is an emphatic position. Rephrase a sentence if doing so forces a key word to the end.

This law is difficult to comply with.
Complying with this law is difficult.

shifts in person

When you write, you adopt a perspective. You can speak from your point of view ("I") or from your company's ("we"), you can address the reader ("you"), or you can write about one or more third parties ("he," "she," "it," "they"). These perspectives are identified as first person, second person, and third person. All three are acceptable. What is *not* acceptable, however, is shifting perspective in a single sentence, or a series of sentences.

Some shifts in person are obvious:

> If an employee works hard, you may be promoted.

The sentence should be consistent, either all in third person or all in second person:

> If an employee works hard, he or she may be promoted. *OR*
> If you work hard, you may be promoted.

In longer passages, shifts in person often go unnoticed:

> Although auditors do not purposely investigate records for fraud, they should be aware of the possibility of fraud. If you suspect fraud, notify a senior auditor immediately.

In this passage the writer shifts from the third person ("the auditors" and "they") to second person ("you"). The second sentence should be revised to be consistent with the first ("If auditors suspect fraud, they should notify a senior auditor immediately"), or the entire passage should be rewritten in the second person:

> Although you will not purposely investigate records for fraud, you should be aware of its possibility. If you suspect fraud, notify a senior auditor immediately.

since, to mean because

Using *since* with the meaning of *because* is acceptable unless using *since* results in ambiguity. The meaning of the following sentence is clear:

> Since I'll be away, I'd like to reschedule the meeting.

But two interpretations of the following sentence are possible:

> Since you resigned, the office has fallen apart.

It can mean (1) "Because you resigned, the office has fallen apart" or (2) "During the time you have been gone, the office has fallen apart." In using *since*, simply make sure that your meaning is unambiguous.

split infinitive

Use of the split infinitive (putting a word between *to* and the verb, as in "to *fully* appreciate" or "to *casually* remark") is much debated in some offices. It is, however, no longer debated among language experts.

Over sixty years ago, in the first edition of *A Dictionary of Modern English Usage,* H. W. Fowler divided the English-speaking world into five groups: "(1) those who neither know nor care what a split infinitive is; (2) those who do not know, but care very much; (3) those who know and condemn; (4) those who know and approve; and (5) those who know and distinguish." In the ensuing six decades, the vast majority of authorities have echoed the words of Fowler, "We will split infinitives sooner than be ambiguous or artificial."

Awkward: *Really* to understand the problem, you should visit the work site.
Natural: To *really* understand the problem, you should visit the work site.

Awkward: Employees want *better* to understand the implications of the plan.
Natural: Employees want to *better* understand the implications of the plan.

The vast majority of sentences sound natural without splitting the infinitive: "The supervisor asked employees to report *immediately* any unsafe conditions." There is, in fact, no great merit in splitting an infinitive unless splitting it makes a sentence clearer or more natural sounding.

subject/verb agreement

The grammatical requirement that subjects and verbs agree (that is, both must be plural or both singular) is usually easy to meet. But here are a few troublesome situations:

Intervening Phrase. Frequently a phrase falls between the subject and verb:

The duties of a manager *(include/includes)* making sure the staff is content. INCLUDE is correct. (Duties. . . include.)

The length of my letters *(vary/varies)*. VARIES is correct. (Length. . . varies.)

Ignore prepositional phrases coming after the subject when deciding which verb form to use. (The prepositions most likely to create confusion are *of, from, for, in, on, to.*) To prevent being distracted by them, you may wish to bracket prepositional phrases (either mentally or physically) so that they do not obscure the structure of the sentence.

None [of the vice-presidents] *has* offered any advice.
A group [of angry stockholders] *is* expected to attend the annual meeting.

Subjects Containing "Or." Occasionally two subjects (one singular and one plural) may be separated by "or":

Either the chairperson or the committee members *(has/have)* to work fast if the deadline is to be met.

When one part of the subject is singular and one part plural, the verb agrees with the part closer to it. Thus, in the example above *have* is correct. It follows, of course, that if the order within the subject is reversed, the verb must be changed:

> Either the committee members or the chairperson *has* to work fast if the deadline is to be met.

Subjects That Follow the Verb. Sometimes the verb appears before the subject:

> After the holidays *(come/comes)* the slump in sales.

Since the delayed subject is *slump,* the verb should be singular—*comes.* In the following sentence, the subject is plural. So too is the verb.

> Enclosed *are* the catalogue and the price list.

Subjects That Look Plural. Finally, some subjects are plural in form but singular in meaning:

> A million dollars *was* too much for that equipment.
> Three hours *is* too long to wait.

that

That may be omitted in a sentence, as long as its meaning is clear:

> Jean knows [that] she has to work hard to be promoted.
> She said [that] she would be willing to work overtime.

But *that* should be retained when its deletion causes misreading, as in the following:

> Chris showed us the report was accurate.
> Ezra said in June he was going on vacation.

In the first instance, Chris didn't show us the report. Rather,

> Chris showed us *that* the report was accurate.

In the second sentence, the meaning is ambiguous. Putting *that* in one of two places clarifies the meaning:

> Ezra said *that* in June he was going on vacation.
> Ezra said in June *that* he was going on vacation.

That may also be used if it improves the rhythm of a sentence:

I think *that* I shall never see
A poem lovely as a tree.

that, which

In deciding whether to use *that* or *which* in a sentence, you must first determine if the group of words introduced by *that* or *which* is essential to the meaning of the sentence or simply supplies extra information. (If the information is essential, it is referred to as a restrictive element. If it is not essential, it is a nonrestrictive element.)

Compare these two sentences:

The house that Jack built is for sale.
The large brown Victorian house, which Jack built, is for sale.

In the first sentence above, the clause "that Jack built" is essential to the meaning of the sentence, for it identifies the house. In the second sentence, the clause "which Jack built" gives additional information about the house but does not identify it.

When the information is essential to the sentence (restrictive), *that* is ordinarily used. No commas are necessary. When the information is supplementary or additional (nonrestrictive), *which* is used. Commas are necessary.

Compare the two pairs of sentences below, noticing how *that* and *which* have been used. Notice, too, where commas have been used.

The policy that covers sick leave has been broadened.
Policy 32A, which covers sick leave, has been broadened.

The company that produces electric golf carts is located next to a golf course.
Carts Inc., which produces electric golf carts, is located next to a golf course.

(Also see the final comma rule on page 125.)

who, whom

The rules regarding *who* and *whom* are not applied as strictly as they once were. Some authorities accept *who* whenever it comes at the beginning of a sentence. Thus, "Who did you see?" is considered an alternative to "Whom did you see?" "Who did he ask for?" is acceptable, though "For whom did he ask?" would be preferred by the purist.

Most of us use *whom* quite naturally when it follows a preposition: "Jim is the person *to whom* the telegram was sent." "Beth is the boss *for whom* I have the most respect." But because using "whom" sometimes sounds heavy or wordy, rephrasing the sentence is often preferable: "The telegram was sent to Jim." "Beth is the boss I most respect."

Sometimes you can't avoid using *who* or *whom*. In these cases you will use *who* or *whom* correctly if you play with the sentence a bit and try substituting *he* or *him* for the troublesome *who* or *whom*. Simply replace the questionable *who(m)*, first with *he* and then with *him*. If *he* fits, use *who;* if *him* fits, use *whom*. Here's how it works:

Questionable sentence:
Tell me *who/whom* will get the job.

Substitutions:
(1) *He* will get the job. (correct)
(2) *Him* will get the job. (incorrect)

Solution:
Tell me *who* will get the job.

It is often necessary to reverse the word order to use the substitution test.

Questionable sentence:
I don't know *who/whom* I should invite.

Substitutions:
(1) I should invite *he*. (incorrect)
(2) I should invite *him*. (correct)

Solution:
I don't know *whom* I should invite.

Alas, not all sentences are quite as easy as those examples:

Questionable sentence:
Give the message to *whoever/whomever* answers the phone.

Substitutions:
(1) *He* answers the phone. (correct)
(2) *Him* answers the phone. (incorrect)

Solution:
Give the message to *whoever* answers the phone.

The trick here is to recognize that *whoever* goes with "answers the phone," *not* with "Give the message to."

Someday the distinction between *who* and *whom* may disappear completely. Who knows?

Punctuation Review

Punctuation marks allow you to indicate in a written passage the pauses, inflections, and stopping places of the spoken language. Your speech pattern, your tone of voice, your self-interruptions come across through the various punctuation marks you use.

The signal system is standard, yet in a few cases there is some room for individual preference. Some writers always insert a comma before *and* in the final item in a series. Others omit the final comma. Some writers use dashes liberally. Others use a less emphatic comma or colon. The system is not totally arbitrary, however. Each mark does serve a specific purpose. If you use the marks properly, your readers will move along, pause, and stop just where you want them to.

Punctuation is not difficult to learn. Besides reviewing the rules, you may find it helpful to observe how punctuation marks are used in major newspapers and magazines. Studying the punctuation in only one paragraph each day will help you master the marks.

The following review presents the major rules that apply to business writing.

apostrophe

The apostrophe has two uses:

- To indicate omission of a letter or number:

  don't   we'll   o'clock   the class of '95

- To indicate possession:

If the possessive word is singular, add an apostrophe and *s:*

  the company's goals   Smith's salary   James's job

(If adding a second *s* makes pronunciation difficult, add only the apostrophe: Moses' commandments.)
If the possessive word is plural and ends in *s*, add just an apostrophe:

  the companies' reports   the accountants' manuals

the Joneses' mansion   three months' delay

If the possessive word is plural and does not end in *s*, add an apostrophe and *s:*

the foremen's complaints   the children's voices

It's easy to get confused. Try flipping the words around, using the word *of*, when you are unsure of yourself. If the *s* is not on the word, add an apostrophe and *s.* If the *s* is already on the word, simply add an apostrophe:

the goals of the company = the company's goals
the reports of the companies = the companies' reports

Do not use the apostrophe with pronouns that are already possessive (*his, hers, its, ours, yours, theirs,* and *whose*):

The book was *hers.*
The company and *its* subsidiary are located in the same building.

Note: The apostrophe was once used to form plurals of numbers and letters (*1970's, P's* and *Q's*). That use has fallen away. No apostrophe is required (*1970s, Ps* and *Qs*) unless adding just the *s* forms a word (*As, Us*). In that case, do use an apostrophe and *s* (*A's, U's*).

colon

Besides its conventional use after the salutation in a business letter, the colon has two other primary uses:

- To introduce a list or a series of ideas:

  The following officers attended the meeting: Leah Chronkite, Maria Rodriguez, Nick Pappas.

In the example above, a complete sentence preceded the colon. The following sentence *needs no colon* because the part before the colon is not a complete sentence:

The new centers will be in Phoenix, Dallas, and St. Louis.

A colon would be needed if a complete sentence preceded the list:

The new centers will be located in these cities: Phoenix, Dallas, and St. Louis.

- To link two closely related ideas or sentences. The information after the colon explains the preceding information:

He went into the meeting with only one thing on his mind: getting a raise.

The cream will have two effects: It will eliminate itchiness and it will reduce swelling.

Note: A phrase or a complete sentence may follow the colon (as in the two sentences above). Use a capital letter after the colon only if a complete sentence follows.

comma

The comma is the most used punctuation mark. There are many rules and many exceptions to the rules. Use the comma in the following ways:

- To separate parts of dates and place names:

April 15, 1996   Portland, Maine   London, England

A comma follows the date and place name when they appear in sentences—unless they end a sentence.

On April 15, 1996, Carl Winters announced plans for a new plant in Portland, Maine, the company's first plant in the Northeast.

When only the month and the year are used, no commas are required:

In March 1995 their plant was damaged by fire.

Note: Because the U.S. Postal Service now uses an Optical Character Reader to sort mail, it asks that no comma be used between the city and state on envelopes or mailing labels that are typed (TUCSON AZ 85710). They also ask that you use no other punctuation, a uniform left margin, and all capital letters. Ask your local post office for Notice 221, "Addressing for Success." This brochure presents the proper format for addressing mail.

- To separate names from titles or degrees that follow:

Paul R. Payton, Jr.
Maria Whitcomb, M.D.
Anthony Cabot, Esq.

In sentences, a comma is required after the title or degree:

Paul R. Payton, Jr., married Maria Whitcomb, M.D., last week.

- To separate items in a series:

a. The trainees were bright, hardworking, and enthusiastic.

b. The job required them to work long hours, to travel for days at a time, and to bring in a stipulated amount of business monthly.

Using the comma before the final *and* is recommended. It can never be wrong and sometimes it prevents ambiguity. If beach umbrellas come in "red, white and blue" you may not be sure if you have two or three choices of color (*red, white and blue* OR *red, white, blue*).

When several descriptive words precede one noun, commas may be unnecessary:

c. The streamlined inventory system allowed them to check the availability of a product within minutes.

An easy way to tell whether a comma is necessary is to substitute the word *and* for the comma. If *and* sounds all right between the words, use the comma. In sentence (a) above, you can say "bright, and hardworking, and enthusiastic"; thus, a comma can be used instead of the word *and,* or in addition to it for the final item. In sentence (c), *and* does not fit between the words. You do not mean "streamlined and inventory"; thus, no comma is used.

- To separate two complete sentences joined by *and, but, nor, or, for, yet* (the comma comes *before* these joining words):

  The clerks wanted to be unionized, and they made that want known to management.
  Management refused to comment publicly, but they argued at length privately.

If the two sentences are very short, no comma is needed:

  They fought hard but they did not win.

- To separate *yes*, *no*, and words of direct address from the rest of the sentence:

  Yes, they did approve the plan.
  Mike, let me know if you want to work with us.

- To separate an introductory phrase or clause from the main part of the sentence:

  After the prototype was produced, it was tested.
  Pleased with the results, management recommended that production begin immediately.
  Because no marketing budget had been allocated, sales were slow initially.

If the introductory expression is short, the comma is sometimes omitted:

> After March we will be using the new system.

- To separate contrasting ideas:

> Kate said $1.5 million, not $1.8 million, was approved.
> It was to be spent for research, not development.

- To set off appositives, that is, a word or words that identify or describe a preceding word:

> Marcia Campbell, our treasurer, will be addressing the group.
> The Omni Group, a consortium of international investors, will publish the newsletter.

- To enclose interrupting or parenthetical information:

> Bart appeared, as one would expect, calm and in control.
> He made a few comments, mainly about production, as I remember.

- To set off a nonrestrictive element. A nonrestrictive element contains additional or nonessential information:

> The president's office, which has large picture windows, overlooks the harbor.
> The office, with its oriental rugs and velvet couches, was recently redecorated.

A restrictive element is essential to the meaning of a sentence. It contains no commas:

> The person who had previously occupied the office was surprised by its new elegance.
> A company that designs and sells fine furnishings has to be well decorated.

(Also see "that, which" on page 119.)

dash

The dash is an emphatic punctuation mark. It indicates a break or shift in thought. The dash signals a pause greater than that signaled by the comma or colon and less than that signaled by parentheses.

The dash can be used to complete the first idea or to express an afterthought:

> The company has but one goal—to become profitable.
> Sam said we'd all get raises—maybe next year or the year after that.

Pairs of dashes can be used in the middle of a sentence to interject a quick interrupting thought or to convey clarifying information:

Herbal Logs—to be introduced next fall—will be a popular item for Christmas.
Two laws—those pertaining to IRAs—came up for discussion.

Pairs of dashes are also used to set off parenthetical elements that contain internal commas:

He said he hoped—but would, of course, not promise—that bonus checks would be given out today.

exclamation point

The exclamation point may be used after emphatic statements and commands. It should not be used, however, as a substitute for a more emphatic word or phrase. Overuse of the exclamation point may make writing seem overly casual or adolescent.

An exclamation point should be used here:

Congratulations! I've just heard about your promotion.

But this sentence should be revised:

Sales for the first quarter increased substantially!
Sales for the first quarter soared 56%.

hyphen

The most common use of the hyphen is to divide a word at the end of a line. Such a hyphen must come between syllables. The hyphen has four other uses:

• To attach some prefixes and suffixes:

prefixes: ex-, quasi-, half-, quarter-, self- (self-interest)
suffixes: -elect, -odd (twenty-odd dollars)

Many words that were once hyphenated are now written without the hyphen:

cooperative   semicolon   reinforce

However, if the root word is capitalized, the hyphen is still required:

un-American   anti-Soviet   post-Vietnam

To be sure of any specific word, consult your dictionary.

- To join compound words:

  eighty-six   cover-up   great-grandmother

The dictionary also shows hyphenated compound words.

- To connect two or more words that have a single meaning:

  long-term debt   out-of-date equipment
  across-the-board raises   state-of-the-art technology

When the words hyphenated in the examples above, or others, are used after the noun, no hyphens are used:

  Raises were given across the board.

- To prevent misreading:

  a dirty-book salesman   a dirty book-salesman

period

The period is used in the following ways:

- After statements, requests, or indirect questions:

  The shipment is to arrive today.
  Please let me know as soon as it gets here.
  Would you also tell Beverly when it arrives.

- After some abbreviations:

  A.M.   P.M.   B.A.   M.A.   Ph.D.   Ms.   Mrs.
  Mr.   M.D.   Co.   Inc.   U.S.A.   U.K.   F.O.B.

But many abbreviations and acronyms are written without periods:

  IRS, MADD, LIFO, HMO, and so on. (See "Abbreviations" on pages 107–108.)

question mark

Use a question mark after direct questions:

  Did he get promoted?
  What will his new title be? Director? Senior partner?

quotation marks

Quotation marks are used in the following ways:

- To enclose direct quotations:

  The chairman has said on more than one occasion, "Our company is not a candidate for takeover. "

But not indirect quotations:

  The chairman has said that our company is not a takeover candidate.

- To enclose titles of essays, articles, television programs, and chapters or sections of longer works:

  "Lock in Those High Rates," written by my partner, appeared on the front page of the business section.

- To denote coined words or words used in a special sense:

  The "bikeathon" will be sponsored next Sunday.
  Technical analysts on Wall Street are sometimes referred to as "gnomes."

Other Punctuation Marks with Quotation Marks. The period and the comma are always placed inside the final quotation mark. The colon and semicolon are placed after the final quotation mark:

  The differences in storage methods are described in the second section of the report, "Safe Storage."
  Temporary dumps, or "hold-dumps," store waste for up to three months.
  Long-term dumps are referred to as "perm-dumps"; however, they are not truly permanent.

When a question mark is used with quotation marks, it may fall inside or outside the final quotation mark. If the quoted material is itself a question, the question mark is placed inside the quotation marks. If the whole sentence is a question, the question mark is placed outside the quotation marks.

  He asked, "Would you consider reducing your fee?"
  Did you tell him "absolutely not"?

semicolon

The semicolon has two uses:

- To connect two sentences that are closely related:

  We have no alternative; we must act now.
  Raises are justified; productivity has risen.
  Profits are down; however, the future of the company is secure.

The third sentence above illustrates the most common use of the semi-colon—that is, when the second complete sentence begins with a word like *however, therefore, thus, consequently, furthermore.* (For a fuller discussion of conjunctive adverbs, see "Comma Splice" on page 110 of the glossary.)

- To connect elements in a series when one or more elements contain commas:

    Please send your comments to one of these committee members: Pat Warner, director; Nilda Falcon, bureau chief; or Wallace Christiansen, project officer.

    The president sought opinions on her plan from the vice-president, who supported it; the treasurer, who opposed it; and a consultant, who recommended further study.

Afterword

Reading Can Help Your Writing

If you read a lot, you will develop a sense for language and for the written word. You will store away, quite unconsciously, patterns, phrases, and rhythms that will help you write better.

Read books, magazines, and newspapers, as well as business correspondence. But read critically. Not every piece of writing is well written. After you have finished reading a memo, letter, or report—or anything, for that matter—ask yourself whether it was clear and easy to read. If it was clear, take a moment to analyze how it was written. If it was not clear, look for places where the writer went wrong. Try to learn from his or her mistakes.

Consult reference books and other books about writing. Skim the books and become familiar with them in your spare time. Then when you're having trouble writing, you'll know which expert to turn to.

The following books are among my favorites:

REFERENCE BOOKS

The American Heritage Dictionary of the English Language, 3rd ed. Houghton Mifflin, 1992. What a wonderful dictionary! It takes the language seriously. Its 173 usage experts are among the most respected guardians of the language.

The Business Writer's Handbook. 4th ed. Charles T. Brusaw and Gerald J. Alred. St. Martin's Press, 1993. If you need a quick answer to a question about different kinds of business documents, or about grammar and usage, this book will provide it.

The New York Public Library Writer's Guide to Style and Usage. Andrea J. Sutcliffe, ed. HarperCollins, 1994. This book is easy to use, easy to understand, and enjoyable. It is comprehensive (800 pages). You won't have to hunt down your answer by using several books. This one book will have it. If your office needs an authoritative source, get a copy of this book.

Roget's International Thesaurus, 5th ed. Robert L. Chapman. HarperCollins, 1992. This classic can help you think of a word that doesn't immediately come to mind. The previous edition (the one most of us have) was copyrighted in 1946. It's time to purchase this new edition, which includes contemporary usage.

BOOKS ABOUT WRITING

The Elements of Style, 3rd ed. William Strunk, Jr. and E.B. White. Macmillan Publishing, 1979. If you enjoy reading about writing, you'll enjoy this classic. It is sophisticated and clever.

Guide to Managerial Communication, 3rd ed. Mary Munter. Prentice Hall, 1992. Although this book provides few examples, it nicely summarizes techniques you can use in planning and preparing written and oral presentations.

On Writing Well, 5th ed. William Zinsser. HarperCollins, 1994. Zinsser does not deal with business writing specifically, but he will help you understand what "writing well" is all about.

Writing That Works, 2nd ed. Kenneth Roman and Joel Raphaelson. HarperCollins, 1992. This practical book is easy to read, and its advice is easy to implement.

A BOOK ABOUT DESIGN

The Non-Designers Design Book. Robin Williams. Peachpit Press (Berkeley, CA), 1994. This short, entertaining book is a primer on design and typographic principles for the visual novice. The book shows writers how to place words on the page for maximum impact.

Index